LESSONS FROM THE PARABLES

LESSONS FROM THE PARABLES

by
Neil R. Lightfoot

BAKER BOOK HOUSE
Grand Rapids, Michigan

© 1965 by Neil R. Lightfoot
Paperback edition issued by
Baker Book House
with permission of
Sweet Publishing Co.

ISBN: 0-8010-5564-4
Library of Congress Catalog
Card No. 65-18264
Printed in the United States of America

Second printing, April 1978

DEDICATION

This book was written with three little girls in mind —

Donna Lynn,
Lu Anne, and
Michelle —

in the hope that they will always remember Jesus' lessons.

FOREWORD

The parables of Jesus will always remain the very center and heart of the teachings of Christ. They summarize what Jesus thought and taught and lived. They tell us what the good life is, what the real values of life are. They speak to man, and bind principles upon him, in terms that he can understand. They are plain, practical lessons for all ages, even as they depict a religion that is designed for all men.

It is fitting, therefore, that many studies have been published on the parables. To many of these I am greatly indebted. I wish to commend especially a recent work on the parables entitled *And Jesus Said: A Handbook on the Parables,* by William Barclay. To his many penetrating suggestions I owe much. My aim throughout has been to consider the lessons in the parables. I have purposefully left unexplored certain theological aspects of the subject on which there has been an increasing interest among recent writers. In keeping with my purpose, I have included only a minimum of notes, although in most cases the reader will find adequate documentation in either the text or the margin. In order that the parables might speak in their original simplicity, quotations of Scripture usually have been taken from the Revised Standard Version. I wish to add that it has been a source of continual inspiration and joy to spend these hours studying again the greatest lessons taught by the Master. It is my prayer that this series of studies will help in drawing all men to Him.

Neil R. Lightfoot

Abilene Christian College
Abilene, Texas

CONTENTS

LESSONS FROM THE PARABLES

1

INTRODUCING THE PARABLES

The parables comprise more than one-third of the recorded teachings of Jesus. The Master of all teachers often put men to thinking by using pictures. He did not leave principles of the Way of life in abstraction, but brought them down within reach of "humble doors." Instead of saying, "Beware of ostentation in religion," He said, "Don't blow a trumpet when you do your giving." This preference of Jesus for vigorous figures of speech results in His frequent use of parables. It has been said that all the world loves a story. Certainly all the world remembers Jesus' parables more than anything else He said.

What Is a Parable?

The word *parable* is a Greek word and literally means "a throwing alongside." One thing is placed by the side of another thing for the purpose of comparison. Thus a parable is a comparison or an analogy. Often a parable is defined as "an earthly story with a heavenly meaning." This is a good expression, but as a definition it is not broad enough to include all the parables. Some parables are not stories. "Physician, heal thyself" (Luke 4:23) is termed a parable by Jesus. We might rather choose to call it a proverb. Jesus' statement "the things that proceed out of the man are those that defile the man" is also called a parable (Mark 7:15-17). It is a kind of riddle that prompts the individual to ask himself: "What is there that comes out of me that is more important than what I take in?" The word parable, then, as used in the Gospels, is a loose term and may mean simply a figurative saying. Yet almost all of the parables of Jesus are comparisons, many of which assume the form of a story.

Jesus' Use of Parables

It is remarkable that the other writers of the New Testament, although they use allegories and similitudes, do not resort to the story-parable as used by Jesus. On occasion, however, the parabolic story is found in the Old Testament. One example is the Parable of the Vineyard in Isaiah 5:1-7. In this parable Israel is compared to a beautiful vineyard. God planted Israel on a fertile hill and expected good fruit, but instead Israel yielded wild grapes. Another parable is recorded in 2 Samuel 12:1-7, and it is the most famous of the Old Testament parables. David had desired Bathsheba, and in order to get her he sent Uriah, her husband, to the front lines to be killed. Nathan the prophet came to David and told him a little story. "There were two men," he said. "One was very rich, with flocks and herds, and the other was very poor. The poor man had only one ewe lamb, but it was a pet of the household and was treated as part of the family. One day a traveler came through; and the rich man, instead of taking from his own flock, took away from the poor man the only lamb he had." David, on hearing the story, was thrown into a violent rage, and said, "The man who would do anything like that deserves to die." And Nathan said to him, "You are the man."

This is the way that Jesus used the parables. By telling a story that was true-to-life, he would draw a parallel between earthly affairs and heavenly things. Jesus knew how well men are acquainted with material matters — a farmer sowing in the springtime and workers at the harvest separating the wheat from the tares, a merchant who gives his life in quest of a rare pearl, or children who play in the marketplace — and using these time-less pictures He sought to tell men about the principles that count in the unseen world. Sometimes He would begin by asking, "What do you think?" or sometimes at the story's end He would turn to His listeners and demand of them a verdict. And surely this is one reason why Jesus spoke so often in parables. He could arouse the curiosity of His audience by beginning a story, and they could follow Him all the way through without realizing where He was leading them. Then all at once the hidden meaning of the story would strike them like a flash, and they could not contradict what He said. This is what happened when Nathan told his parable. The sins of David had lulled his conscience to sleep, and without knowing it David judged his own case and rightly pronounced the death-sentence against himself.

Interpreting the Parables

It is impossible to lay down strict rules for the interpretation of the parables, for the amount of comparison varies from parable to parable. In the Parable of the Sower, for example, small details in the story, even the birds and the sun, are important; while in the Parable of the Prodigal Son, such things as the fatted calf and "the music and dancing" obviously have no meaning. When studying the latter parable it would be foolish to ask, "What do the swine stand for?" or "What does the ring on the finger represent?"

A failure to recognize that all of the details of a parable are not meaningful has led many astray in their interpretations. It is important to distinguish between a *parable* and an *allegory*. An allegory, like a parable, is a story told in order to make a comparison. In an allegory every detail of the story has an inner meaning. The Apostle Paul used an allegory of two women, Hagar and Sarah, to contrast the Old and New Covenants (Galatians 4:24-31). In this allegory Paul explained that Hagar represents Mount Sinai or the Old Covenant, while Sarah represents the Jerusalem above or the New Covenant. Likewise, every other detail in this allegory corresponds to something. But in a parable — and this is the main difference between a parable and an allegory — each detail is not necessarily significant. The details of a parable are there most often just to add color to the story.

In ancient and medieval times it was customary to treat the parables of Jesus as allegories. An early Christian scholar named Origen, who lived in the third century, may be cited as an illustration. His interpretation of the Parable of the Good Samaritan is as follows: The man who fell among robbers is Adam. Jerusalem represents heaven, and Jericho, since it was away from Jerusalem, represents the world. The robbers are man's enemies, the devil and his comrades. The priest stands for the Law; the Levite for the prophets; and the Good Samaritan for Christ Himself. The beast, on which the wounded man was placed, is Christ's body which bears the fallen Adam. The inn is the Church, while the two pence are the Father and the Son. The Good Samaritan promises that he will come back again, so Christ Jesus will come again at the end of the world. The whole thing is a rather ridiculous interpretation, but for many centuries this is the kind of interpretation that was offered for the parables. Even Richard C. Trench of the last century, whose work on the parables is still valuable for its intro-

ductory chapters, is not exempt from this fatal mistake of allegorizing the parables.[1]

The *first* rule in interpreting the parables, then, is to find out the
central truth which the parable sets forth. The question must always be asked, "What is the main lesson of the story?" When once
the main truth of the parable is grasped, then all of its related
truths are to be evaluated with reference to the whole framework.
If the Parable of the Sower mainly illustrates how the Word of God
is received, all of the other parts of the parable are to be understood
in this light. Common sense must apply here, as in interpreting any
portion of Scripture.

The *second* rule is to understand the parable in light of the
circumstances of its origin. The background of the parable and the
context of the passage in which it appears will help immeasurably
in understanding it. It may be that a parable will have more than
one object in mind. Indeed, the contexts of some of the parables
suggest that several lessons are to be learned. In the Parable of the
Sower, which is very much like an allegory, Jesus clearly intends to
provoke thought on a number of things that pertain to the Kingdom. Even so, the context of the passage gives Jesus' own interpretation and supplies the meanings of a story that would otherwise
be very obscure.

Distribution and Arrangement of the Parables

It is difficult to say how many parables are present in the Gospels.
The exact number depends on one's definition of a parable. If the
word *parable* is taken to include proverbs, riddles, and simple comparisons as well as those in story form, the number is about sixty
in all. Not counting all of these, the number of parables is usually
estimated as being from thirty to thirty-five.

For some strange reason the Gospel of John does not use the

---

[1]One example of this is found in Trench's exposition of the Parable of the
Talents. According to him, the servants primarily were the apostles; the gifts
received were the spiritual powers bestowed on them; the time of the giving
was the day of Pentecost; and the master's going away was the Lord's ascension.
This interpretation, however, occasions conflict, for in the parable the master
distributes the gifts before he goes away. This would make Pentecost take
place before the ascension. Trench, of course, is aware of the problem, but
still approaches the passage allegorically. See Richard Chenevix Trench, *Notes
on the Parables of Our Lord* (London: Macmillan and Co., 1882), pp.
273, 275.

word *parable*, although a word of similar meaning is employed.[2] This means that in order to locate the parables of Jesus it is necessary to go to Matthew, Mark, and Luke. Only a few parables appear in Mark, for it is characteristic of Mark to devote his record more to the deeds of Jesus than to His words. In Matthew and Luke are to be found most of the parables. Luke in particular preserves not only the majority of Jesus' recorded parables, but also those of exceptional beauty and appeal.

Below is one list of the parables and their locations in Scripture.

PARABLES RECORDED IN MATTHEW, MARK, AND LUKE

	Matt.	Mark	Luke
Children of the Bridechamber .	9:14-15	2:18-20	5:33-35
New Patches on Old Garments .	9:16	2:21	5:36
New Wine in Old Wineskins .	9:17	2:22	5:37-38
The Sower	13:3-23	4:2-20	8:4-15
The Mustard Seed	13:31-32	4:30-32	13:18-19
The Wicked Husbandmen . .	21:33-45	12:1-12	20:9-19
The Fig Tree	24:32-33	13:28-29	21:29-31

PARABLES RECORDED IN MATTHEW AND LUKE

	Matt.	Luke
The Wise and Foolish Builders	7:24-27	6:47-49
Children in the Market Place	11:16-17	7:31-32
The Leaven	13:33	13:20-21
The Lost Sheep	18:12-14	15:3-7
The Wise Steward	24:45-51	12:42-48

PARABLES RECORDED IN ONLY ONE GOSPEL
In Matthew

The Tares	13:24-30
The Hidden Treasure	13:44
The Precious Pearl	13:45-46
The Dragnet	13:47-50
The Householder	13:51-53
The Unmerciful Servant	18:23-35

[2]The term used by John is *paroimia,* which is well translated by the Revised Standard Version as *figure.*

THE PARABLE OF THE SOWER

"That same day Jesus went out of the house and sat beside the sea. And great crowds gathered about him, so that he got into a boat and sat there; and the whole crowd stood on the beach. And he told them many things in parables saying: 'A sower went out to sow. And as he sowed, some seeds fell along the path, and the birds came and devoured them. Other seeds fell on rocky ground, where they had not much soil, and immediately they sprang up, since they had no depth of soil, but when the sun rose they were scorched; and since they had no root they withered away. Other seeds fell upon thorns, and the thorns grew up and choked them. Other seeds fell on good soil and brought forth grain, some a hundred fold, some sixty, some thirty. He who has ears, let him hear. . . . Hear then the parable of the sower. When any one hears the word of the kingdom and does not understand it, the evil one comes and snatches away what is sown in his heart; this is what was sown along the path. As for what was sown on rocky ground, this is he who hears the word and immediately receives it with joy; yet he has no root in himself, but endures for a while, and when tribulation or persecution arises on account of the word, immediately he falls away. As for what was sown among thorns, this is he who hears the word, but the cares of the world and the delight in riches choke the word, and it proves unfruitful. As for what was sown on good soil, this is he who hears the word and understands it; he indeed bears fruit, and yields, in one case a hundredfold, in another sixty, and in another thirty.'"

(Matthew 13:1-9; 18-23)
(Parallel passages: Mark 4:1-8, 13-20;
Luke 8:4-8, 11-15)

2

THE RESPONSIBILITY OF HEARING

According to Mark the first word of this story is "Listen!" The story concludes on the same note with the commanding words: "He who has ears, let him hear." It is well known that the man who teaches has much responsibility, but Jesus is saying here that the man who hears also has responsibility. Hearing is a serious matter. It is not to be taken lightly. Watch out *how* you hear is the key-note to the parable.

Jesus' Early Parables

This parable was spoken by the Sea of Galilee and in the vicinity of the town of Capernaum. It was one of the early parables of Jesus, but probably was not His first. On a previous occasion Jesus was challenged as to why His disciples did not fast. He responded to His critics with a parable. "Can the wedding guests mourn," He said, "while the bridegroom is with them? But when the bridegroom has gone away, then they will fast and mourn" (Matthew 9:15). Two other short parables follow. "No one puts a new patch on an old garment," said Jesus, "nor do men put new wine into old wineskins" (Matthew 9:16-17). These three parables teach the same lesson. It is absurd to think that a woman would sew an unshrunk patch on an old garment, or that a man would put unfermented wine in old skins that were about to break. So it is ridiculously absurd to expect Jesus' disciples to fast while He is still with them. These are some of Jesus' earlier parables which preceded the Parable of the Sower.

The Four Kinds of Ground

The story about a sower as he sows seed was a familiar picture to Jesus' audience. The sower went out into the field and scattered his seed abroad; and the seed fell on different kinds of ground. First, there was the wayside ground. In Palestine the land was divided up into small plots. There were no fences or walls to separate the plots, only narrow paths that were accessible to everybody. Due to frequent traffic they were well worn, and seed dropped on these hard walkways had little chance for growth. Second, there was the rocky ground. The rocky ground was not that which was full of rocks, but ground that was shallow due to an underlying ledge of rock. It had no depth. The seed when sown here would spring up quickly, but in the heat of summer would wilt and die out. Third, there was the thorny ground. This ground was not already covered with thorns, but had an abundance of weed-seeds buried underneath the soil. The weeds came up with the good seed, and the strong weeds outgrew and overcame the delicate good plants. Fourth, there was the good ground. It was fertile and loose and able to receive the good seed. It had depth enough to allow the roots to go down and it was clean enough to allow unhindered growth.

One Possible Interpretation

In recent years one interpretation of this parable has received increasing favor. It goes like this. By the time the parable was spoken, opposition to Jesus was already mounting; and even with His great following it was becoming more and more clear that many of the people who pressed about Him were not genuinely interested in spiritual values. The disciples were on the verge of overwhelming discouragement. Thus Jesus seems to acknowledge to them that much of the sower's efforts will go for nothing, that in the sowing of seed it is not expected that all of it will make a crop. And yet the parable is reassuring to the disciples: no matter how much is wasted, in the end there will be a plentiful harvest. The sower must never be disheartened.

The Sower and the Seed

The four kinds of ground are the focal points of the story, but other features in the parable are important as well. The sower is a representative of a group; he stands for anybody who is engaged in the sowing business of the kingdom. He is the gospel preacher or the Bible teacher or anyone who talks to his friend about Christ. The seed which is sown is the Word of God (Luke 8:11). Everyone knows how important seed is. Life is impossible without seed. Likewise, apart from the Word of God new life is impossible (see 1 Peter 1:23; James 1:18). The pure seed of the kingdom when received in good soil always produces Christians.

The Soils and the Human Heart

Jesus' interpretation of the parable hinges on the four kinds of ground. The story takes for granted that the seed sown by the sower is good, so whether or not the seed bears fruit depends on the type of soil into which the seed falls. The four different kinds of ground, then, represent four different conditions of the human heart.

1. *The wayside ground.* This ground is so hard that the seed cannot possibly enter it. Some people who hear are like this. They hear the message of the kingdom, but the message is wasted. It may be that as they hear they allow their minds to wander about in idleness; or they may hear, like the Pharisees, with arrogance and pride, and turn away in ridicule and scorn; or they may hear with their eyes on others, always applying the lesson to someone else. After hearing the message they go away, and their lives are just as they were before they heard. The hard, pathway soil represents the individual whose mind is closed. He shuts his eyes and refuses to look, he stops his ears and will not listen.

Is the soil to blame because it is hard? Yes, if the soil is the human heart. Sin is what sears the conscience and hardens the heart (see Hebrews 3:13). A human heart can be hardened like pavement by persisting in wrong and rejecting the right. A heart once aglow with love can become insensitive to the needs of others by failing to take advantage of opportunities for doing good. Each refusal to do God's will is like a hundred steps on the human heart, and for this every individual is accountable. Each man is the cultivator of his own heart.

2. *The rocky ground.* There were many people who followed Jesus impulsively and at times ran over Him in order to get to Him. What was wrong with them? It was not that they accepted Jesus too readily, for one cannot be too quick in doing what is right. It was not that they were too enthusiastic. Their trouble was that their faith was shallow. It was thin, like a thin layer of soil over a bed of rock. When persecution came, they gave it all up. Their faith was outward instead of inward.

The description is true-to-life. Some people accept the gospel quickly, and lay it aside just as quickly. They live on their feelings rather than on their convictions. Some people, for example, are so absorbed in the preacher that when he moves away they lose their faith. Cities and towns are full of those who accepted Christ before they thought things through. Many people have found out that it is not easy to be a Christian, although it is easy to start.

3. *The thorny ground.* This stands for the person who is so busy with other things that he cannot be busy for Christ. Life sometimes gets that way. Thorns grow up before we know it. What are the thorns? Jesus explains them as being "the cares of the world, the delight in riches, and the lust for other things" (Mark 4:19). And this may be summarized simply as the concerns for life on earth. It is not that earthly things are necessarily bad in themselves. Many times they are not. Good things can occupy a person's time as well as the bad, and more often than not it is these good things that drain our energies and turn our hearts away from Christ. *A thorn is anything that crowds Jesus out of our lives.*

If it was necessary that Jesus present a lesson in His day on the thorns, how much more so is it today. We stand in danger of being choked to death! We are so busy; we do not have time for prayer and study and quietude. Our lives are cumbered by this and that until the good within is smothered out. No matter how strong we are, we cannot serve two Masters (Matthew 6:24); and not even the best of us is able to produce a crop of wheat and a crop of thorns at the same time. Thorns can be weeded out, and that is exactly what Christ demands of us in order that His cause might be our first interest in life.

4. *The good ground.* The three Gospel accounts explain the meaning of the good ground. In Matthew 13:23 it is said that the good hearer *understands* the word. He hears it, he follows it through from beginning to end, and he does not stop thinking about it until he really knows its meaning. In Mark 4:20 the good hearer is described as one who *receives* the word. This means he takes it in and it becomes a part of him. In Luke 4:15 the good hearer is said to be the one who *keeps* the word; he holds on to it and practices it in his life. Luke adds that the good hearer brings forth fruit "with patience" (8:15). He does not expect a harvest overnight. The seed is sown and it takes time to grow. While it is true that a person can experience the new birth almost instantaneously, the person who is truly Christ-like grows and develops in His image. His heart continues to be open and receptive. He seeks to hear not what is easy or popular but what is true. The more patience he has, the more understanding he obtains.

Which kind of ground represents you? Is it possible that your heart is growing hard like the beaten track of the pathway? Or do you find your faith resting more on emotions than on convictions? Is your life filled with so many things that your Christian vitality is in danger? Or are you bearing with patience good fruit that looks forward to the harvest? What kind of fruit is the soil of your life producing?

THE PARABLE OF THE SEED GROWING OF ITSELF

"And he said, 'The kingdom of God is as if a man should scatter seed upon the ground, and should sleep and rise night and day, and the seed should sprout and grow, he knows not how. The earth produces of itself, first the blade, then the ear, then the full grain in the ear. But when the grain is ripe, at once he puts in the sickle, because the harvest has come.' "

(Mark 4:26-29)

3

THE GROWTH OF THE KINGDOM (I)

This parable is found only in the book of Mark. It appears in a series of parables on the kingdom, the more complete record of this series being preserved by Matthew (chapter 13). Its location and content indicate that it should be studied along with the Parable of the Sower. The theme of this parable, as those of the Mustard Seed and the Leaven, is the growth of the kingdom.

The Kingdom of God

Eleven of Jesus' parables are introduced by some such expression as "the kingdom of heaven is like." It is essential, therefore, to learn something about the kingdom that Jesus spoke of so frequently.

The idea of the kingdom of God has its root in the Old Testament. From the beginning the people of Israel are described as being the unique and chosen people of God. They are the recipients of His special favor, and God Himself is their King. Once when the people wanted Gideon to rule over them, he said, "I will not rule over you, and my son will not rule over you; the Lord will rule over you" (Judges 8:23). Later, when the people desired a king, God told Samuel: "They have not rejected you, but they have rejected me from being king over them" (1 Samuel 8:7).

God gave them a king, even though they had rejected Him. Yet as time went on, the more devout and discerning recognized no other dominion than God's. "The Lord has established his throne in the heavens, and his kingdom rules over all" (Psalm 103:19).

The height of the Israelite kingdom was reached in the days of David and Solomon. Those wonderful days of prestige and power were short-lived; and when the Israelite kingdom was on the decline, and still later when it no longer existed, the Israelites looked back fondly to their glory of the past. So the prophets announced that the time would come when the Lord would reaffirm His kingly reign and restore to honor the people called by His name.

God promised that in that day He would raise up "David" as

king, who would be the Messiah (Jeremiah 30:9). It was the
throne of David that was to be permanently established (Isaiah
9:6-7), and the kingdom of David, God's kingdom, was to stand
forever (Daniel 2:44). With this hope the Jewish nation looked
forward to the time when God in a mighty way would interrupt
history, bringing about the fulfillment of His promises. With the
coming of Jesus that time is fulfilled: Jesus preaches that the kingdom of God is at hand (Mark 1:15).

The Kingdom in the New Testament

Different terms are used in the Four Gospels to portray the
kingdom. Most often it is called "the kingdom of God" (Matthew
19:24; Mark 9:1; Luke 17:21; John 3:3). Sometimes it is the
kingdom of "the Son of Man" or the kingdom that belongs to Christ
(Matthew 16:28; John 18:36). Sometimes it is the kingdom of the
Father (Matthew 13:43). Often it is simply the "kingdom"
(Matthew 4:23).

Matthew's favorite descriptive term for the kingdom, and he is
the only writer to use it, is "the kingdom of heaven." This does
not mean "the kingdom *in* heaven." It may denote, however, one
of several ideas. It may mean simply "a kingdom *from* heaven."
Or it may have a descriptive force, a "heavenly kingdom." Or it
may mean no more than "God's kingdom." It is well known that
the Jews would not pronounce the Divine Name; instead they
sometimes substituted the word "heaven." Thus Matthew's "kingdom of heaven" would be the exact equivalent of "kingdom of
God."

The word "kingdom" literally means "reign" or "rule," but it is
used in different senses in the New Testament. It is used in a
present sense and as such equals the church, the body of Christ.
The Apostle Paul speaks of being transferred out of the kingdom of
darkness into the kingdom of God's Son (Colossians 1:13). In Hebrews 12:28 we read of "receiving a kingdom that cannot be
shaken." It is not possible to be transferred into Christ's kingdom
or to receive a kingdom that is not a present reality. The word
kingdom is also used with a *future* reference. In Matthew 25:31
Jesus says that when the Son of Man comes in His glory, "then he
will sit on his glorious throne." In one sense the kingdom is yet
future, for the Son of Man has not yet come in His glory. There
awaits at the end a rich entrance into "the eternal kingdom of our

Lord and Savior Jesus Christ" (2 Peter 1:11). Thus when the kingdom is mentioned in a future sense, it refers to heaven itself.

How the Kingdom Grows

The kingdom is not something that sprang up in a moment. It was planned, prepared for, and brought into being in the past and even now awaits its final consummation. This is the central truth taught in the Parable of the Seed Growing of Itself. The kingdom spreads over the world by growth; and in the growth of the kingdom the parable presents several lessons.

1. *The growth of the kingdom is gradual.* In the production of grain, nature works step by step. Nearly all of its marvels are wrought gradually. It is not hard to detect the result of growth, but the process of growth is imperceptible. So it is with the growth of the kingdom of God — first the blade, then the ear, then the full head of grain ripe in the ear.

Applied to the individual, the parable is a lesson on patience. Christian growth is gradual. If it is possible to expect too little of ourselves, it is possible also that sometimes we expect too much of ourselves. In our moral and spiritual development we want to take giant steps, and if we fail we are sorely disappointed. We forget nature's lesson, the necessity of gradual growth. No scientist is made in a day. No one learns a new language overnight. Millions thrill to the artistry of a great musician in concert, yet very few know anything of the long road of struggle that has led the musician to greatness. If this is true of human things, it is much more true of divine things. One does not go to bed a sinner and wake up a Christian. Men must be taught the way of Christ, and rarely are they brought to Him with one word. Mature congregations of the church of the Lord likewise do not spring up over night. They must be planted and nurtured and developed. So if we are learning, we need to know that learning does not come in the flash of a moment. If we are teaching, we should remember that the human mind is so constituted that only by patient and persistent efforts can the Word of God come to rule the hearts of men.

2. *The growth of the kingdom is orderly.* When the seed is sown and buried in the soil, its very existence seems to be threatened. Yet the little blades appear; then comes the ear; and finally the full grain. The growth of a plant is marked by an orderly development. It is that way with a tree: first the bud, then the blossom, and finally the fruit. It is that way with human beings — infancy,

childhood, youth and manhood. It may be impossible to tell when one period ends and another begins, yet the different stages of growth can be clearly recognized.

In the life of the Christian distinct stages of development are observable. Recent converts are described as being newborn babes who should desire the spiritual milk of the Word for their growth (1 Peter 2:1-3). Others may not be new converts, but tragically may not have grown beyond the baby stage (1 Corinthians 3:1-4). Still others attain maturity or perfection (Philippians 3:15), which should be the ambition of all Christians (1 Corinthians 14:20; Matthew 5:48). So in the Christian life there are different levels of spiritual achievement. A genuine recognition of this will go far in helping to understand fellow Christians. The man who has just begun in the Christian way often needs a considerate look and a helpful hand; and it may be that the best way to understand the irksome brother is that he has not yet grown up in Christ. In Christian growth we should not expect the ear before the blade.

3. *The growth of the kingdom is from God.* No one can explain how things grow. A seed may be taken into a laboratory and analyzed, but the scientist cannot tell what makes a seed turn into a flower. A farmer can do many things to the soil. He can plow it; he can fertilize it; and often can weed it out after the seed is sown. But he cannot make the seed grow. He sows the seed, and wisely "sleeps and rises, night and day," leaving the rest up to God. There are some things that God alone can do.

In the spiritual kingdom, whatever growth takes place is due to the operation of God. The sower may sow his seed, but he cannot make it germinate in the human heart. He can select his seed and prepare the soil, but he cannot make the seed grow. At Corinth, Paul planted; Apollos watered; but it was *God* who gave the growth (1 Corinthians 3:6).

There is danger in overstressing this truth. The power and work of God can be emphasized to the neglect of the ability and duty of man. Man indeed has a vital part in the growing process, and his part is an *active* one. Men cannot make seed grow, but they can see to it that conditions are right so the seed will have a chance to grow. But in the end the kingdom belongs to God, and the growth of the kingdom will be from God. A carpenter who builds a house can make it take shape with his two hands. But the kingdom is *not* like that. A farmer can plant his seed, but he cannot make it grow without the rain and sunshine that come from God. The kingdom *is* like that. The sower must sow his seed and wait patiently for God to do His part. Scripture says, "Behold, the farmer waits for the precious fruit of the earth, being patient over it until it receives the early and the late rain" (James 5:7). Christians must likewise be patient. "You also be patient. Establish your hearts, for the coming of the Lord is at hand" (James 5:8).

This parable, then, is one that puts us in our right place. We are helpless without God. It is not enough to work. The Christian must work and pray. Some things he can do, but there is much that he can never do.

> The Lord is good to those who wait for him,
>   to the soul that seeks him.
> It is good that one should wait quietly
>   for the salvation of the Lord.
>   (Lamentations 3:25-26)

THE PARABLE OF THE MUSTARD SEED

"Another parable he put before them, saying, 'The kingdom of heaven is like a grain of mustard seed which a man took and sowed in his field; it is the smallest of all seeds, but when it has grown it is the greatest of shrubs and becomes a tree so that the birds of the air come and make nests in its branches!'"

(Matthew 13:31-32)
(Parallel passages: Mark 4:30-32; Luke 13:18-19)

THE PARABLE OF THE LEAVEN

"He told them another parable. 'The kingdom of heaven is like leaven which a woman took and hid in three measures of meal, till it was all leavened.'"

(Matthew 13:33)
(Parallel passage: Luke 13:20-21)

4

THE GROWTH OF THE KINGDOM (II)

In addition to the Parable of the Seed Growing of Itself, Jesus gave two other parables on the growth of the kingdom. These two, the Parable of the Mustard Seed and the Parable of the Leaven, look at the same subject from different points of view. The Parable of the Mustard Seed is taken from the garden or field; the Parable of the Leaven is taken from the home.

The Parable of the Mustard Seed

In Palestine it was common to speak of the mustard seed as the smallest of all seeds. Strictly speaking it was not, for there are other seeds that are smaller, but the tiny mustard seed was proverbially used to stand for anything infinitesimally minute. Jesus once spoke of faith as a grain of mustard seed. He told the apostles that if they had faith, even a small amount of faith like a grain of mustard seed, they would be able to do many mighty works (Matthew 17:20; Luke 17:6).

Both Matthew and Mark emphasize that the small mustard seed becomes the largest of the herbs. The Palestinian mustard plant, because of its size, was not set out in the garden but in the open field. It was not unusual for it to grow as high as ten or twelve feet. It was a giant of the shrubs, so large that its branches spread out like a tree. Such a shrub would attract many birds. This is what happened in the parable. In Jesus' time birds could often be seen in the branches of the mustard plant as they fed on the small black seeds of the mustard pods. Thus the parable presented a familiar scene to the Jews, a scene portrayed by Jesus to teach new lessons on the growth of God's kingdom.

1. *The importance of little things.* One of the unmistakable lessons of the parable is the importance of little things. How small is the microscopic mustard seed, and yet how valuable! The little mustard grain by itself does not look so important, but experience

teaches a man not to minimize it. So the little things of life should not be discounted.

The world today is thirsting for bigness. Modern skyscrapers dwarf the tower of Babel. Cities already bulging with factories and people are everywhere seeking more industries and bigger populations. A farmer or a business man is termed a success or failure according to the bigness of his operations. To a world obsessed with magnitude, Jesus says, "Pay attention to the little things." A cup of cold water, a visit to the sick, a welcome to a stranger, a lost sheep — these are little things; but like a grain of mustard seed they increase in size to unimaginable proportions.

2. *Small beginnings.* However important little things may be, the parable actually focuses attention on the consequence of little beginnings. It is a fact that generally the world's biggest things have had small beginnings. The greatest works of art begin with a few strokes of the brush. The world's great symphonies and concertos are based on a few notes. In literature, every book, every essay, every poem, comes from the twenty-six letters of the alphabet. Momentous deeds and earth-circling revolutions can be traced back to a speck like a germ of a mustard seed.

History's greatest movement had its beginning at a manger in Bethlehem. The proud and busy Roman world did not take notice of the day when Jesus was born. Still less did it care when He died, for He was only a carpenter of Nazareth. Certainly in outward appearance Jesus looked "less than the least of all seeds." His followers were counted by the dozens and not by the thousands. And yet from only a handful of disciples, and in spite of their leader's death on a cross, there sprang into existence the universal church of the Lord Jesus Christ. Therefore, we should learn well the lesson of the grain of mustard seed. A thing may begin very small, almost without hope, and still in the end succeed because God is behind it. Did the first-century disciples ever dream of the effect of their faith? Their faith began unnoticed, like a tiny mustard seed, but nevertheless has gone around the world.

3. *The branches of the tree.* One popular conception of the parable is to interpret the branches of the mustard tree as symbolical of modern denominations. Just as the birds come and sit in the branches of the tree, so it is said that people come and enter the different branches or denominations of the church. But there are difficulties attached to this interpretation. First, this view seeks to understand the parable by looking at the Christianity of today instead of Christianity as found in the first century. It is easy today

to speak of "branches of the church," but in the days of Christ and the apostles these divisions were unknown. Did this parable remain without its full meaning until the recent rise of denominationalism? Second, this interpretation stretches the parable too far. It is not necessary to make each detail in a parable stand for something. Attempting to do so results in the fallacy of "allegorizing" the parables. The branches of the mustard tree are not in the main focus of Jesus' attention any more than the man who sowed the mustard seed or the nests that were made in the tree's branches. The point of the parable is simply that the microscopic mustard seed grows into a tree large enough for the birds to come and nest in it. The man who sowed the seed, the field or garden, the nests, the birds themselves, are incidental to the one central truth of the parable — that the kingdom of God even with a small beginning would prosper and prevail over other kingdoms. This is in keeping with Daniel's interpretation of Nebuchadnezzar's dream (Daniel 2:31-45). The stone not cut by human hands struck the image down and became "a great mountain and filled the whole earth." In the same way God's kingdom was destined to conquer all other kingdoms.

The Parable of the Leaven

Many times Jesus had seen women making bread. Everybody knew about it. So He said that the kingdom was like leaven placed in three measures of meal. There is nothing especially significant about the three measures. Probably Jesus mentioned three measures because this was the ordinary amount of meal used in a single baking. Some commentators of the past, however, have allegorized the parable and have made the three measures stand for the three sons of Noah, or the body, the soul, and the spirit of man.[1] Such suggestions typify how far astray some interpretations of the parables have gone. They clearly illustrate how a parable can be sorely misunderstood by attempting to find a parallel for every point in the story. In ancient times leaven as a separate ingredient was not available as it is today. In the leavening of bread, dough was kept over from a previous baking and inserted in the new mixture to ferment it. In the New Testament leaven is used as a symbol of both good and evil. The Jews identified fermentation

[1]These interpretations were offered by Augustine, Jerome and Ambrose, and were unfortunately admired by Trench. See Trench, *Notes on the Parables of Our Lord*, pp. 119-20.

with rottenness, and thus leaven was often used by them to refer to an evil influence. Thus Jesus warned His disciples against the leaven of the Pharisees and of Herod (Mark 8:15); and Paul said on several occasions, "A little leaven leavens the whole lump" (1 Corinthians 5:6; Galatians 5:9). But leaven was likewise used by the Jews to represent a good influence. Standing either for good or bad, leaven was a figure for any strong and pervasive influence.

In this parable Jesus speaks of leaven in the good sense, as a woman uses it for a good purpose to make light and wholesome bread. So understood, the kingdom is like leaven in several respects.

1. *The inner influence.* Leaven does its work from within. It can do nothing to the dough until it is put inside. The religion of Christ works that way. The true influence that changes men works within a person's heart. Men cannot be lifted up by mere external improvements. A poverty-stricken nation may receive food and clothing and better housing, but that nation will not really be changed until it is given something within. Likewise, a man is not converted unless he is converted within — until his heart is changed. Christianity is like leaven. It is not on the outside trying to get in, but it is on the inside trying to get out.

2. *The changing quality.* When leaven is put in the baking-meal, it changes the ingredients. When Christ and His kingdom are introduced to men, great changes take place. Christianity is a disturbing thing. It upsets people. At Philippi, it was said of Paul and his friends, "These men are Jews and they are disturbing our city" (Acts 16:20). At Thessalonica, against the same men, the cry was, "These men who have turned the world upside down have come here also" (Acts 17:6). So it has always been. When Christ comes into a man's heart, he becomes a new man. He does new deeds (Colossians 3:5-17). He has new thoughts (Colossians 3:1-4). He has new ambitions of work and service (Matthew 20:26-28). In short, he is a new creation (2 Corinthians 5:17). The leaven of Christ has transformed his life.

3. *The contagious characteristic.* Leaven works contagiously "until the whole is leavened." It is aggressive. It does not stop until it has spread through the whole mixture. The kingdom of God, likewise, spreads by contagion. Some of Jesus' first disciples were brought to Him by others. Andrew found Peter, Philip found Nathanael, and so on (John 1:40-45). The early church multiplied by leaps and bounds because "each one won one."

The church today is in the soul-winning business, and the only way it can do its business is for every member to be a soul-winner.

Leaven is used in the Scriptures for either good or bad. A good example is contagious like leaven, but a bad example is contagious also. Jesus said that God's kingdom grows and spreads like leaven. Is your influence contributing to that growth?

THE PARABLE OF THE HIDDEN TREASURE

"The kingdom of heaven is like treasure hidden in a field, which a man found and covered up: then in his joy he goes and sells all that he has and buys that field."

(Matthew 13:44)

THE PARABLE OF THE PRECIOUS PEARL

"Again, the kingdom of heaven is like a merchant in search of fine pearls, who, on finding one pearl of great value, went and sold all that he had and bought it."

(Matthew 13:45)

5

TRUE VALUES

Here are twin parables that are brief and penetrating. As Jesus tells the two stories, it is clear that He approves of the actions of both men. One man accidentally stumbled upon a treasure buried in a field. The other found a pearl of great worth, but he found it only after a long and constant search. Both men made once-in-a-lifetime discoveries, and each man gladly exchanged everything he owned in order to buy the object of his devotion. Jesus points to these men and says, "These men know how to use life. They know what is really worthwhile. They recognize values when they see them."

The Parable of the Hidden Treasure

The story of finding a buried treasure was not an unlikely one in the time of Jesus. Back then there were few places of safety where money could be deposited, so often the best place to hide treasured possessions was in the ground. It will be remembered that in the Parable of the Talents the man who had the one talent, wanting to keep it safe, covered it up in the ground. In the parable at hand a man had buried his treasure for safety's sake, but for some reason he was never able to return and recover what belonged to him. Afterward, someone else came across the treasure. The discoverer was overjoyed. What should he do? He decided that he would cover it back up, go and buy the field, and then the treasure would unquestionably be his.

To some people the parable poses a moral problem. Was the man truly honest in his dealings? Would it be right to find a treasure and buy the field without telling the owner what was concealed in it? The difficulty, however, is not as great as it might seem. In the first place, Jewish law at that time expressly stated that anything found, whether money or other goods, belonged to the finder.[1] In this case, then, the treasure *did* rightfully belong to the man. In the second place, and more important, to inquire into all the legalities of the question is to make the mistake once again of carrying the parable too far. The main object of the parable is the finding of the treasure and the willingness to give up everything for it. In the same way Jesus teaches that men should surrender everything for the kingdom of God.

Three Lessons. When this parable is studied and thought through, several lessons stand out clearly. These are conveyed in the treasure, the sacrifice, and the joy.

1. *The treasure.* Jesus tells us that the kingdom of heaven is like a treasure, that it is a treasure, that it is the most wonderful of all treasures. Its value is supreme. It is worth everything and every effort. Men quite generally ignore this. How few are those who believe with all their hearts that the kingdom is a treasure. Theoretically, to be sure, the kingdom is acknowledged as valuable. Many people will confess that they ought to be seeking the kingdom. They know that it offers something that they do not have. Many others will admit that at times the kingdom is of vast value. In time of extreme need, in the midst of days of sickness and when death draws on, people want Christ and His kingdom to be near. To them, at that time, it is a real treasure. But if the kingdom is valuable once, if it is ever valuable, then it is always valuable.

2. *The sacrifice.* The man who finds the treasure "goes and sells all that he has and buys that field." He makes the necessary sacrifice. He knows that things worthwhile are not obtained for nothing. He will pay the price, whatever it is. So it should be with every person who seeks the kingdom. If the kingdom is truly a treasure, treasures are not gotten for nothing. The first requirement for a follower of Christ is self-denial. "If any man wants to come after me, let him deny himself . . ." (Matthew 16:24). Discipleship demands denial.

3. *The joy.* "In his joy he goes and sells all that he has." The word "joy" must not be overlooked. It is a key to the parable. It is significant that the man does not regret selling all that he has in order to get the field. He does not complain about the sacrifice that he has to make. He gave much for the field, but he gets more

---

[1]See Alfred Edersheim, *The Life and Times of Jesus the Messiah* (Grand Rapids: Wm. B. Eerdmans Publishing Company; reprinted in 1947), I, 595-96. This is an older work, but still a valuable one. The point of legality is neglected by many recent writers.

in return. The pain of parting with his goods is lost in the joy of the treasure. This man's joy is the kind of joy a person should have when he gives himself to Christ. A man who is genuinely converted does not grudgingly give up the past. He gives up his past life for something far better. The Apostle Paul is a good example. He said: "But whatever gain I had, I counted as loss for the sake of Christ. Indeed I count everything as loss because of the surpassing worth of knowing Christ Jesus my Lord. For his sake I have suffered the loss of all things, and count them as refuse, in order that I may gain Christ" (Philippians 3:7-8). These are words of confidence and joy. Paul had become Christ's, and Christ had become Paul's; and even though he suffered the loss of all things, he never looked back the second time. The joy that he found in Christ far excelled the joy that he had without Him.

The Parable of the Precious Pearl

The pearl in ancient times was a gem of great delight. Pearls had a high value in terms of dollars and cents. It is reported that Cleopatra had two precious pearls, worth $400,000 apiece. Beyond their money value, pearls were desired in themselves. They held a fascination for the Oriental mind. Simply to look at a pearl, to hold it, to turn it through the fingers, was considered a source of great satisfaction. Pearl merchants looked far and wide for new pearls. Jesus tells of one of these merchants who spends his life in quest of the perfect pearl, and on finding it sells everything and buys it.

The Pearl Merchant and the Kingdom. There is something about the pearl merchant that is attractive. Here in this man are traits of character that are worthy of imitation. What are the qualities in him that appeal to us, and those of which Jesus gave His hearty approval?

1. *He is a man with a definite purpose.* He knows exactly where he is going and what he is looking for. His goal is to find the perfect pearl. With this goal he lived a full and happy life. So it is with us. Too many people today live aimlessly. Wandering about without a proper sense of direction, they rob themselves of the joy of living. But the pearl merchant was possessed of a single eye. He had a sense of direction and of destination. And Jesus congratulates him as he pursues his business with dedicated ambition!

2. *He is a man with the highest possible purpose.* It is not enough with him that he lives a purposeful life, but he has pointed his life in the highest direction possible. He is seeking a priceless jewel. Although he has other pearls, they are not good enough. He cannot be content with second-best. He must have the best. He is seeking, therefore, the values of life that are supreme. And this is precisely what Jesus expects of every man. Some men seek meanness and wickedness; their thoughts are evil continually. But the majority are not that way. That which threatens most men is the danger of giving themselves to trifling things, to things in the long run that are of no importance. They risk much of the big business of living in search of glittering nothings. But the teachings of Jesus condemn this quest for the trivial. He plainly says that the greatest objective of life is the heavenly kingdom. "Seek first his kingdom and his righteousness, and all these things shall be yours as well" (Matthew 6:33). All other things, even food and clothing, must be secondary (Matthew 6: 25-34). The pearl merchant was in quest of the best. Nothing secondary satisfied. So we must make certain that the quest to which we give our lives is worthwhile.

3. *He is a man who is willing to pay the necessary price for the perfect pearl.* Of course this is to say that he knows values when he sees them. He has that rare ability of being able to approve what is excellent (see Philippians 1:9-10). Being a good judge of values, he buys the pearl. He knows that his life-time of searching would all be in vain unless he buys it. He did not simply wish that he had the pearl, as some people admire Christianity and wish that they were Christians. Nor did he degrade the pearl's value, as a worldling makes light of the rewards of Christianity. Neither did he wait for the price of the pearl to come down, as some people tragically think that later on in life it will be easier to follow in the footsteps of Christ. No; he acts swiftly. "How much do you want for the pearl?" he asks. And he is not at all surprised to learn that its price is very great. So he rushes off to sell all his pearls to buy the one pearl. He freely gives up the second-best that he might have the best.

The pearl that he bought was the object of his life. His years of searching would have been in vain if he had not bought it. What did it matter if he had to sacrifice everything for it! When we come to Christ, we give Him everything. He is the Pearl of Great Value. And things of great value are only obtained at great cost.

THE PARABLE OF THE TARES

"The kingdom of heaven may be compared to a man who sowed good seed in his field; but while men were sleeping, his enemy came and sowed weeds among the wheat, and went away. So when the plants came up and bore grain, then the weeds appeared also. And the servants of the householder came and said to him, 'Sir, did you not sow good seed in your field? How then has it weeds?' He said to them, 'An enemy has done this.' The servants said to him, 'Then do you want us to go and gather them?' But he said, 'No; lest in gathering the weeds you root up the wheat along with them. Let both grow together until the harvest; and at harvest time I will tell the reapers, gather the weeds first and bind them in bundles to be burned, but gather the wheat into my barn. . . .'"

"Then he left the crowds and went into the house. And his disciples came to him, saying, 'Explain to us the parable of the weeds of the field.' He answered, 'He who sows the good seed is the Son of man; the field is the world, and the good seed means the sons of the kingdom; the weeds are the sons of the evil one, and the enemy who sowed them is the devil; the harvest is the close of the age, and the reapers are angels. Just as the weeds are gathered and burned with fire, so will it be at the close of the age. The Son of man will send his angels, and they will gather out of his kingdom all cause of sin and all evildoers, and throw them into the furnace of fire; there men will weep and gnash their teeth. Then the righteous will shine like the sun in the kingdom of their Father. He who has ears, let him hear.'"

(Matthew 13:24-30, 36-43)

THE PARABLE OF THE DRAGNET

"Again, the kingdom of heaven is like a net which was thrown into the sea and gathered fish of every kind; when it was full, men drew it ashore and sat down and sorted the good into vessels but threw away the bad. So it will be at the close of the age. The angels will come out and separate the evil from the righteous, and throw them into the furnace of fire; there men will weep and gnash their teeth."

(Matthew 13:47-50)

6

THE MIXTURE OF GOOD AND BAD

Here again are two parables that should be studied together. Both of them deal with the coexistence of good and evil, and both teach that, although good and evil may stand side by side for awhile, eventually a great and permanent separation will be made between them.

The Parable of the Tares

The Parable of the Tares tells the story of a farmer who prepared his field and sowed it with good wheat-seed. After this a malicious enemy slipped in at night and sowed tares on top of the wheat. At first no one knew about it; and by the time the evil trick was discovered, nothing could be done except wait for harvest.

Wheat was a very important crop and was grown in most parts of the land of Palestine. There were several varieties of tares or darnel, the one most probably referred to in the parable is called "bearded darnel." This darnel was a poisonous rye-grass which was very common in the East. It looked very much like wheat, and in its early stages of growth was practically impossible to distinguish from wheat.[1] But as soon as the grain began to head, the difference was obvious. By that time the wheat tares had grown so close together that any effort to weed out the bad would damage the good.

William Barclay has listed three ways by which the tares were separated from the wheat.[2] If the tares were few, which was not the case in this parable, women and children were put to the task of picking out the bad seed from the good before the grain was milled. Or, when the tares did not grow as tall as the wheat, sometimes the wheat was harvested over the top of the tares and

---

[1] The ancient Jews believed that this darnel, technically known as *Lolium temulentum*, was a kind of degenerate wheat (*Kilaim* 1:1).

[2] William Barclay, *And Jesus Said: A Handbook on the Parables of Jesus* (Edinburgh: Church of Scotland Youth Committee, 1952), p. 37.

then the field of tares was burned. Or the tares and the wheat were separated by the reaper at the harvest, the reaper preserving the good grain but stacking up the tares to be burned.

Interpreting the Parable. Jesus Himself outlines the meaning of the parable: the field is the world; the sower of the good seed is the Son of man; the sower of the tares is the devil; the good seed are the sons of the kingdom; the bad seed are the sons of the evil one; the reapers are the angels; and the harvest is the end of the world. But in spite of this explanation the parable still is regarded as difficult. One problem is how to understand the statement of the householder. Of the mixture of the wheat and the tares, he says: "Let both grow together until the harvest." What does this mean? Can it possibly be taken in the sense, as many have done in the past, that wicked people in the church are not to be disciplined? The answer to this question is found in another statement of the parable. Jesus said that "the field is the world." The parable, then, is not talking of good and bad in the church but of good and bad in the world. This being the case, it could not bear even remotely on the question of church discipline.

But with this explanation another problem arises. Jesus says, "The Son of man will send his angels, and they will gather out of his kingdom all causes of sin and all evil-doers." What does Jesus mean by this statement? Does the word "kingdom" here refer to the church? If so, are there not then good grounds for thinking that the parable touches on church discipline? It is true that many times the term kingdom in the New Testament denotes the church. A familiar example is found in Matthew 16:18-19, where evidently the words "church" and "kingdom" are used interchangeably. This does not argue, however, that in every passage the word kingdom must point exclusively to the church. The important factor to keep in mind is the relation of the context itself to the application of the word. In the parable the field where the good and bad seeds were sown, and the kingdom out of which the bad were gathered, are obviously the same. A man would not sow in one field and gather out of another. But Jesus said that "the field is the world"; therefore, in this passage the kingdom is the world. This is an unusual meaning for the word kingdom, but it is not without parallel. In at least one other passage, the Parable of the Pounds, the word kingdom includes both the Lord's willing subjects and those who were His enemies (Luke 19:12-27). In the Parable of the Tares, likewise, the kingdom embraces both the good and the bad of the whole world. So here the kingdom is not the church, and thus it remains true that the parable is misinterpreted if applied to church discipline.

Lessons of the Parable

1. *The existence of evil.* There are such things in the world as tares. The world is not like a perfect wheat crop. It may bear good wheat, but wherever the good wheat grows the tares are growing also. Christianity has had a vibrant effect on the world, and yet no nation or state, no city or village, is wholly Christian. Nor are the most mature congregations and the best homes thoroughly Christian. No matter where one looks, he can see tares. It is a perplexing problem, but the Lord has taught us that it is characteristic of this life and will always be.

The source of the tares is the Evil One. When the servants ask where the tares came from, the householder replies simply, "An enemy has done this." Jesus explains that this enemy is the devil. It is worth noting that Jesus believed in and taught the existence of an evil personality known as the devil. According to Jesus, there is a wicked power at work among men which is opposed to God. Conceive of it however you will, call the devil whatever you like, still the Bible teaches the reality of sin and the presence of temptation (see 1 John 1:7-10; 1 Corinthians 10:13; 1 Timothy 6:9). Still the Bible reads that "he who commits sin is of the devil" (1 John 3:8), and that "the wages of sin is death" (Romans 6:23).

2. *The impossibility of judgment.* It will be remembered that much of the significance of the parable lies in the close resemblance of the wheat and the tares. It was practically impossible to distinguish between the two. So this parable is a kind of commentary on Jesus' statement, "Judge not, that you be not judged" (Matthew 7:1). It makes it clear that men do not have the ability to judge between the good and the bad. It means that in the end the judgment of others is a divine and not a human function.

The trouble with man is that he is too limited. He sees only the outward appearance. When the prophet Samuel came to Bethlehem to anoint a king, he looked favorably upon one of Jesse's sons and said to himself, "Surely this is the Lord's anointed." But the Lord said to him, "Do not look on his appearance or on the height of his stature, because I have rejected him; for the Lord sees not as man sees; man looks on the outward appearance, but the Lord looks on the heart" (1 Samuel 16:6-7). Outward appearances are often deceiving. Time and time again our first impressions have proved to be wrong. Frequently we say of people that we have known for years, "Well, I didn't know that about him." There is much that we do not know about our most intimate acquaintances. There is even much undiscovered knowledge about ourselves. In the final analysis, hardly any of us would pretend to be able to pass final judgment on others. How many of us would be willing to name over our friends and say, "This one ought to go to heaven, and that one ought to go to hell"? It is only in a very limited way that men are able to judge. At most man is able to acquire only a few facts. He should not presume to judge beyond his limited and tentative findings. As one man has said, "God Himself does not propose to judge a man till he is dead. So why should I?"

3. *The separation of good and evil.* Although the wheat and the tares grow together for a time, when harvest comes they are completely and finally separated. Thus the parable is a parable on judgment. Man *is not able* to judge, but God *will* judge. The time of harvest is certain to come. And then the counterfeit wheat will be gathered and burned.

The Parable of the Dragnet

This parable is generally known as the Parable of the Dragnet. The dragnet was a seine-net used often by the fishermen on the Lake of Galilee. It was a large net, with weights on the bottom and floats on the top. As it swept through the waters, fish of all kinds were sucked in its path. The net was then drawn to land, and the fishermen sat down on the shore to sort their catch. The good fish were put in vessels and taken to the market to be sold. But the rough and waste fish were thrown away.

Like the parable of the wheat and the tares, this too is a parable on judgment. One can picture in his mind a group of fishermen as they go through their fish, placing the good on one hand and the bad on the other. The disciples were well acquainted with the routine. To them Jesus says, "Just as you put the good fish aside and keep them, and throw out the bad, so it will be in the Day of Judgment. The good and useful will be saved; the bad and useless will be cast away."

Fish are either good or bad. What is not wheat is weeds. Jesus teaches in these two parables that men are either good or bad and that there is no "in between."

THE PARABLE OF THE TWO DEBTORS

"One of the Pharisees asked him to eat with him, and he went into the Pharisee's house, and sat at table. And behold, a woman of the city, who was a sinner, when she learned that he was sitting at table in the Pharisee's house, brought an alabaster flask of ointment, and standing behind him at his feet, weeping, she began to wet his feet with her tears, and wiped them with the hair of her head, and kissed his feet, and anointed them with the ointment. Now when the Pharisee who had invited him saw it, he said to himself, 'If this man were a prophet, he would have known who and what sort of woman this is who is touching him, for she is a sinner.' And Jesus answering said to him, 'Simon, I have something to say to you.' And he answered, 'What is it, Teacher?' 'A certain creditor had two debtors; one owed five hundred denarii, and the other fifty. When they could not pay, he forgave them both. Now which of them will love him more?' Simon answered, 'The one, I suppose, to whom he forgave more.' And he said to him, 'You have judged rightly.' Then turning toward the woman he said to Simon, 'Do you see this woman? I entered your house, you gave me no water for my feet, but she has wet my feet with her tears and wiped them with her hair. You gave me no kiss, but from the time I came in she has not ceased to kiss my feet. You did not anoint my head with oil, but she has anointed my feet with ointment. Therefore I tell you, her sins, which are many, are forgiven, for she loved much; but he who is forgiven little, loves little.' And he said to her, 'Your sins are forgiven.' Then those who were at table with him began to say among themselves, 'Who is this, who even forgives sins?' And he said to the woman, 'Your faith has saved you; go in peace.'"

(Luke 7:36-50)

7

LOVE AND FORGIVENESS

Jesus had received an invitation to dinner from Simon. We do not know when or where the dinner was held, except that it was in the house of a Pharisee. Others too were invited guests, which implies that Simon had attained a respectable economic and social level in his community. The poor people of Palestine lived in very small houses, ordinarily consisting of only one room. Those who were wealthy lived in houses of several rooms adjoining an open courtyard. The courtyard, of course, was a favorite spot, and in the heat of summer was commonly the place where meals were served. In those days people did not sit in upright chairs while eating. The tables were built close to the floor and were surrounded by low couches. The usual eating position was to recline on the left side and rest on the left elbow; this allowed the right hand to move easily during the eating of the meal. Reclining in leisure while eating was a custom the Jews had borrowed from the Greeks. The original Greek word *kataklino*, translated "sit at table," literally means to "lie down" or "recline."

The Characters of the Story

The first character to notice is Simon. He was a Pharisee. The name Pharisee literally means "the separated one." The Pharisees were the *Purists* or the *Separatists* of their day, the strictest party of the Jewish religion (see Acts 26:5). It was not so much their strict observance of the law but their binding of petty regulations about the law that restricted them from others. The Pharisees were aloof from everything non-Jewish. They separated themselves also from the mass of the people, the vulgar crowd, which they called "the people of the land." Yet Simon the Pharisee invited Jesus to dinner. We do not know why. Possibly he extended the invitation in order to find fault in Jesus, or perhaps he was simply curious and wanted to find out more about Him. Whatever the explanation, the parable itself shows that Jesus was not invited out of a heart of friendship and love.

The woman in the story is unnamed and unknown. There is no reason to identify her with Mary Magdalene or Mary the sister of Lazarus. We know only that her sins were many. It is better that she remain in obscurity.

The Progress of the Story

A woman with a notorious reputation comes in and takes a position behind Jesus. She begins to weep. Her tears fall upon His feet and she wipes them with her long hair. In that time it was considered immodest for a woman to undo her hair in public, but this woman's love for her Lord is overwhelming and she is oblivious to the outcome of her actions. She had brought with her a jar of precious perfume which she uses to anoint Jesus' feet; and as if this were not enough, she lavishes her love upon Him by kissing His feet.

From the beginning, it seems, Simon and his friends were suspicious of Jesus. And now that all this has transpired, they sat there in amazement. Simon says to himself: "This is enough to convince me. If this man were a prophet, he would know that this woman is a shameful sinner and would have nothing to do with her." But love understands love, and so Jesus says, "Simon, I have something to say to you. Once there was a man who had two debtors. One owed five hundred denarii, and the other owed fifty denarii.[1] Neither of the debtors was able to pay his debt, and the man forgave them both. Now Simon, which of the two will love him most?" Simon could only reply, "I suppose the man to whom he forgave more." It was then that Jesus revealed to Simon the difference between himself and the sinful woman. Simon had not extended to Jesus even the routine courtesies which were given a guest — no water for His feet, no oil for His head, and no kiss of love. But the woman, whom Simon looked upon with disdain, overflowed in the expression of her appreciation and love.

The Lessons of the Story

1. *Christ's love for us.* The first thing that strikes us about this story is Christ's willingness to receive the affection of a corrupt woman. The woman was a known sinner. The Pharisees would

---

[1]The denarius was a Roman coin worth about twenty cents.

have nothing to do with the common people, much less a person who was the worst in the lot. And it is to be remembered that the whole scene was enacted in public before the eyes of those who were quick to criticize. In those days it was an unheard of thing for a rabbi to speak to a woman in public, and the liberties this woman took with Jesus were doubly shocking to the dinner guests. Jesus knew the kind of woman she was, and even so He was not ashamed or embarrassed by her conduct. "If this man were a prophet," they said, — they expected Him either to know better or to do better. Jesus knew, and therefore He could not have acted more wisely.

Thus one of the highlights of this lovely story is that Christ receives sinners. The most beautiful lines in the Gospels are those that tell with what sympathy and tenderness the Lord handled the down-trodden and the outcasts. At Sychar a Samaritan woman confronted Him. Although she had wrecked her life by many marriages, He talked kindly with her about eternal life; and surely it was His method as much as what He said that brought her to faith in the Messiah (John 4:7-30, 39-42). It was a trade-mark of Jesus that He was a friend to the tax-collectors and sinners. Sometimes today men do not come to Christ because of their sins. They wait, trying to cleanse themselves in order to be worthy of Christ's love. But self cannot cleanse that which only the blood of Christ can cleanse (Ephesians 1:7; 1 Peter 1:18-19). Jesus' enemies ridiculed him because He received sinners, but today it is still His highest glory.

2. *Our love for Christ.* This story teaches us that our love for Christ is in proportion to our consciousness of sin. There was a radical difference between Simon the Pharisee and the sinful woman. Simon was not aware of his sins, but the woman could never forget that she was a sinner. Simon was a man who did not need forgiveness; the woman was one who needed much forgiveness. The difference between the two, then, was basically a consciousness of sin and a need for a Savior.

It is a misapplication of the parable to suppose that one must be forgiven of great sins in order to have a great love for Christ. Nevertheless it is true that a man who has spent thirty years behind prison walls can appreciate his freedom more than a man who has spent only one night in jail. And this is the way it often is with sin and forgiveness. Some people have experienced the famine of sin for years, and for them it is a great and constant joy to be in Christ. Yet this does not mean that we should continue in sin that grace may abound (Romans 6:1-4). One who is truly seeking forgiveness cannot at the same time be loving sin. Often the worst sinner is void of conscience and cannot feel sin, while the purest and the best are always conscious that they fall short of God's glory. So in the end it is not the *amount* of sin but it is the *awareness* of sin that makes a man *appreciate* his Savior. Until we learn what Christ has done for us, Christ will not be dear to us.

3. *The greatest of these is love.* This story also teaches us the greatness of love. Jesus asked Simon which of the two men would love his creditor more. Why did He ask this question? Clearly because love is so important. The sinful woman, with all her faults, had love; and love was the main thing that was lacking in the life of self-sufficient Simon. All of Simon's scrupulous observance of the Pharisee's traditions could not replace love.

Jesus said that the first command of the kingdom is to love God with all one's self, and that the second command is to love man as one's self (Mark 12:29-31). Love is basic. It is both first and second. Nothing is worthwhile without it. Love sustains all.

> Love is very patient, very kind.
> Love knows no jealousy; love makes
> no parade, gives itself no airs, is
> never rude, never selfish, never irritated,
> *never resentful;* love is never glad
> when others go wrong; love is glad-
> dened by goodness, always slow to
> expose, always eager to believe the
> best, always hopeful, always patient.
> Love never disappears.
>
> (1 Corinthians 13:4-8;
> Moffatt's translation)

The parable teaches that our love for Christ is no greater than our appreciation for pardon. But appreciation for pardon depends on our conviction of sin. We cannot make light of sin and be grateful for salvation. Perhaps this is the root of the problem in world-wide evangelism. We appreciate our own forgiveness too little, so we have only a little to share with the world.

THE PARABLE OF THE UNMERCIFUL SERVANT

"Then Peter came up and said to him, 'Lord, how often shall my brother sin against me, and I forgive him? As many as seven times?' Jesus said to him, 'I do not say to you seven times, but seventy times seven.

" 'Therefore the kingdom of heaven may be compared to a king who wished to settle accounts with his servants. When he began the reckoning, one was brought to him who owed him ten thousand talents; and as he could not pay, his lord ordered him to be sold, with his wife and children and all that he had, and payment to be made. So the servant fell on his knees, imploring him, "Lord, have patience with me, and I will pay you everything." And out of pity for him the lord of that servant released him and forgave him the debt. But that same servant, as he went out, came upon one of his fellow servants who owed him a hundred denarii; and seizing him by the throat he said, "Pay what you owe." So his fellow servant fell down and besought him, "Have patience with me, and I will pay you." He refused and went and put him in prison till he should pay the debt. When his fellow servants saw what had taken place, they were greatly distressed, and they went and reported to their lord all that had taken place. Then his lord summoned him and said to him, "You wicked servant! I forgave you all that debt because you besought me; and should not you have had mercy on your fellow servant, as I had mercy on you?" And in anger his lord delivered him to the jailers, till he should pay all his debt. So also my heavenly Father will do to every one of you, if you do not forgive your brother from your heart.' "

(Matthew 18:21-35)

8

LOVE AND MERCY

The steps leading up to this parable have been preserved by Matthew. Jesus had been talking about right relationships among the disciples, that if one brother sinned against another, the brother wronged should go and talk to him about his fault (see Matthew 18:15-17). These admonitions from Jesus put Peter to thinking; and so he comes up and says, "Lord, what I want to know is, *how often* should I forgive my brother? As many as seven times, is that enough?" Peter surely felt that he would be complimented by the Lord, for he was willing to forgive more than most people. The Jewish rabbis at one time taught that a man was to be forgiven three times, but no more.[1] Peter multiplied this number by two, added one for good measure, and then patted himself on the back and said, "Look what a wonderful fellow I am to be willing to forgive like that!" Peter indeed was willing to forgive, but his mistake was that he measured himself by a human rather than a divine standard. So Jesus says to him, "Not just seven times, Peter, should you forgive your brother, but seventy times seven." An alternative in translation is "seventy-seven times" instead of "seventy times seven." At any rate the meaning is the same, for Jesus was teaching that a person should always be ready to forgive. It is not a problem of *counting* but a problem of *conduct*.

The Story Told

There is not much in the parable itself that needs explanation. A king called all of his servants in to settle accounts, and he found that one man owed him ten thousand talents. This was a fantastic sum of money; and there simply was no excuse for

---

[1]The Babylonian Talmud reads: "Rabbi Jose ben Jehuda said, If a man commits an offense once they forgive him, a second time they forgive him, a third time they forgive him, the fourth time they do not forgive him" (*Joma* 86b).

a man to squander that much in a lifetime. So the king commanded that he be sold, with his wife, children, and all of his possessions, in order that payment might be made. This was in keeping with the Mosaic law (see Exodus 22:3), and the servant knew it. Thus he fell down and begged for mercy, and the king forgave him all his debt. Immediately the same servant went out and found a fellow servant who owed him a hundred denarii. The debt was not large, about twenty dollars, and granted a reasonable period of grace, undoubtedly could have been met. And yet, notwithstanding the begging of the servant, the small sum of money owed, and the pardon that he himself had received from the king, the servant would not forgive his fellow servant. The other servants naturally were embittered and went and told the whole story to the king. When the king learned of what had happened, he summoned the heartless servant in and told him he should have forgiven his fellow servant just as forgiveness had been bestowed on him — that because he had not been merciful, he would receive no more mercy. So it will be, Jesus said, with every one who does not forgive his brother from his heart.

The Story Understood

The primary lesson of the parable stands out bright and clear: if a man receives pardon from God, he has the obligation to extend pardon to his brother. This is the central impact of the story. The parable is so rich and meaningful, however, that it emphasizes other truths as well.

1. *The nature of human judgment — condemning.* One of the first things that leaps out from the parable is the heartless way the servant treated his fellow servant. He took him by the throat. In Greek and Roman custom a debtor was taken by the throat and brought to court to stand trial. The Greeks spoke of choking the life out of a person and meant by it that they were making him pay his debt. Grasping him by the throat he insisted, "Pay what you owe!" He made it a matter of principle, as if to say, "Honest people pay their debts." We can picture him saying this with the utmost of piety, as he holds his fellow servant by the throat with the hand so soon released from prison chains. The scene is painfully humorous.

The unmerciful servant expected from his fellow what he did not expect from himself. How easy it is to see others' failures. Mistakes in others are sins; in us they are only faults. What is meanness in others is mischief in ourselves; what is harshness in others is frankness in ourselves; what is selfishness in others is thrift in ourselves. In the work of the church, we often expect much more of others than we will do ourselves. We expect others to take the lead, others to do the work, and we are quick to criticize if they do not. We need to remember the teaching of Jesus on condemning judgment (Matthew 7:1-5). A man with a big plank in his own eye need not be so concerned about a speck of sawdust in his brother's eye. If only we were as gentle and understanding and kind to others as we are to ourselves!

2. *The nature of divine forgiveness — merciful and just.* In the parable the king who owns everything is God; the debt is sin; and the servant stands for every man. As the king could not hold back his pity from the servant who had wasted his money, so God the Father is merciful to all. "For with the Lord there is steadfast love, and with him is plenteous redemption, and he will redeem Israel from all his iniquities" (Psalms 130:7). "Though your sins are like scarlet, they shall be as white as snow; though they are red like crimson, they shall become like wool" (Isaiah 1:18). "As far as the east is from the west, so far does he remove our transgressions from us" (Psalms 103:12). "If we confess our sins, he is faithful and just, and will forgive our sins and cleanse us from all unrighteousness" (1 John 1:9). God is willing to forgive us of all of our sins.

Although God is merciful to us, He is also just in forgiveness. The heart of the parable is that God will not forgive us of our sins unless we freely forgive others. Thus the parable enshrines two great principles stated in the Sermon on the Mount. First, "Blessed are the merciful, for they shall obtain mercy" (Matthew 5:7). Forgiving others is truly a Christian grace. The law of Moses did not obligate man to forgive his fellow. Forgiveness of enemies was not regarded as a virtue in Israel. But Jesus taught that forgiveness is a duty. No offense is so great or so frequent as to be beyond forgiveness. "If your brother sins, rebuke him, and if he repents, forgive him; and if he sins against you seven times in the day, and turns to you seven times, and says 'I repent,' you must forgive him" (Luke 17:3-4). "Be kind to one another, tenderhearted, forgiving one another, as God in Christ forgave you" (Ephesians 4:32). So we are to forgive one another, as often as seven times in a day, as much as seventy times seven. This does not mean that sin is to be ignored or overlooked. To the contrary, the person who sins is to be rebuked and the person who repents is to be forgiven. God does not pass over sins lightly, nor should man. Nevertheless the man who has no pity for his fellow will not get pity from God.

The second principle of the Sermon on the Mount enforced here is, "Forgive us our debts, as we have forgiven our debtors" (Matthew 6:12). "As we have forgiven our debtors" (found in the American Standard and Revised Standard Versions) is a more exact translation, making it clear that we must forgive others *before* we can be forgiven. It is wonderful to proclaim the fact of divine forgiveness, but the condition of divine forgiveness must be underscored as well. God forgives *as* we have forgiven. If we address God with hatred and bitterness in our hearts, if we pray to God knowing that we are at odds with a brother, we are making it impossible for Him to forgive our sins. Robert Louis Stevenson had the custom of praying the Lord's Prayer every day in family worship. One day as he came to these words in the prayer, he stopped and said, "I cannot pray that prayer today." We should be on guard against empty phrases in prayer, and we need to be especially thoughtful before repeating the Lord's words, "Forgive us our debts, as we have forgiven our debtors." A man once said to John Wesley, "I never forgive!" Wesley responded, "Then I hope, sir, that you never sin." God's forgiveness and man's are inseparably joined.

3. *The nature of human debt to the divine — unpayable*. The parable plainly teaches that all men are debtors to God. There is no difference here, there is no exception. "All have sinned and fall short of the glory of God" (Romans 3:23). "All we like sheep have gone astray; we have turned every one to his own way" (Isaiah 53:6). Man's relationship to God, then, is one of debtor to creditor. We owe Him more than we can ever pay. The two sums of money owed in the parable are deliberate extremes. The servant owed his fellow servant a hundred denarii. The denarius was a Roman coin worth about twenty cents, which made the total debt about twenty dollars. But the servant owed the king ten thousand talents. It is difficult for the casual reader to grasp how large an amount that was. The talent was worth approximately $960.00; then ten thousand talents would equal $9,600,000.00. It was a staggering sum, an unimaginable figure. It is said that Judea, Idumea, Samaria, Galilee and Perea brought in annually about eight hundred talents in tax money.[2] The debt

---

[2]George A. Buttrick, *The Parables of Jesus* (Garden City, New York: Doubleday, Doran and Company, Inc., 1928), pp. 99-100.

was much more than all the tax money of several provinces. It was a debt that no one could pay. So it is with our obligation to God. How much do we owe the Lord? Some people do not feel that they owe Him anything. They breathe God's air, devour His sunshine and rainfall, yet never give Him a passing glance or one ounce in return. Other people acknowledge that they owe the Lord *something*, while others confess that they owe the Lord *much*. But this parable smacks at our vanity and self-reliance and says to each of us, "You owe the Lord much more than you can ever pay." What are we able to give to God? Shall we give Him cattle? The cattle on a thousand hills belong to Him (Psalms 50:10). Shall we give Him our life-long service? Even so, we are still worthless servants who have done no more than our duty (Luke 17:10). So if our debt to God is enormous, and if we have nothing really with which to discharge our obligations, then salvation is of divine grace and not of human merit. Here we are debtors and beggars, all.

A Parable of Contrasts

In summary, this parable is striking and impressive because of its acute contrasts. First, there is the contrast of Peter's number and the Lord's. Peter was willing to forgive seven times, but the Lord said to forgive to infinity. Second, there is the contrast of the two debts. One was a trifling sum, the other was unpayable. Likewise, the wrongs done to us and the injuries we receive from our fellows are infinitesimally small in comparison with the magnitude of our sins against God. Third, there is the contrast of the creditors. The mighty king forgave, but the lowly servant would not. If God is willing to forgive the more, we should be willing to forgive the less.

The servant got into trouble after he was forgiven. Have you been forgiven? If so, what are you doing with your forgiveness?

THE PARABLE OF THE GOOD SAMARITAN

"And behold, a lawyer stood up to put him to the test, saying, 'Teacher, what shall I do to inherit eternal life?' He said to him, 'What is written in the law? How do you read?' And he answered, 'You shall love the Lord your God with all your heart, and with all your soul, and with all your strength, and with all your mind; and your neighbor as yourself.' And he said to him, 'You have answered right; do this, and you will live.'

"But he, desiring to justify himself, said to Jesus, 'And who is my neighbor?' Jesus replied, 'A man was going down from Jerusalem to Jericho, and he fell among robbers, who stripped him and beat him, and departed, leaving him half-dead. Now by chance a priest was going down that road; and when he saw him he passed by on the other side. So likewise a Levite, when he came to the place and saw him, passed by on the other side. But a Samaritan, as he journeyed, came to where he was; and when he saw him, he had compassion, and went to him and bound up his wounds, pouring on oil and wine; then he set him on his own beast and brought him to an inn, and took care of him. And the next day he took out two denarii and gave them to the innkeeper, saying, "Take care of him; and whatever more you spend, I will repay you when I come back." Which of these three, do you think, proved neighbor to the man who fell among the robbers?' He said, 'The one who showed mercy on him.' And Jesus said, 'Go and do likewise.' "

(Luke 10:25-37)

9

LOVE AND NEIGHBORLINESS

Jesus' story of a traveling Samaritan who gave aid to a wounded stranger is a story that has left an indelible imprint on the conscience of mankind. Luke is the only writer who records these words of Jesus. Were it not for him, this most beautiful story could not be re-told.

The Lawyer's Question

On several occasions the question of what one should do to inherit eternal life was put to Jesus (see Matthew 19:16-22; 22:35-40, and parallels). This time the question was raised by a lawyer. The lawyer by profession was an expert in the Jewish law. He was a man who was supposed to know all the answers. So Jesus asked him, "What is written in the law? How do you read?" — as if to say, "You are an expert in these matters. You of all people should be able to answer your own question." And the lawyer had a ready answer. He quoted from Deuteronomy 6:5 and Leviticus 19:18 and showed that the law required perfect love for God and perfect love for man. "You are right," said Jesus. "If you keep the law as well as you quote it, you will have eternal life." But the lawyer's original question was not asked with pure motives; and when Jesus' reply put him on the spot, he sought a way of escape by asking, "Who is my neighbor?" The lawyer's struggle at self-defense is met with an earnest illustration on true neighborliness.

The Road and Its Travelers

The road connecting Jerusalem and Jericho is famous for its many danger spots. Jerusalem is situated in the hills, about 2,300 feet above sea-level; and Jericho is located on a low plain near the Dead Sea, about 1,100 feet below sea-level. The road between the two cities covers only seventeen miles but descends about 3,400 feet. Winding, turning, dropping sharply, the zig-zag path has proved to be a hazardous one through the centuries. Josephus in the first century described it as "desolate and rocky";[1] and in the late fourth century Jerome spoke of it as a road infested with bandits.[2] W. M. Thomson, for thirty years a missionary to that region of the world, has preserved something of the daring adventure that attended a journey from Jerusalem to Jericho. In the year of 1833, as related in his *The Land and the Book*, he made this very trip, beginning from St. Stephen's Gate in the eastern wall of Jerusalem. His description of the trip is as follows: "We passed out St. Stephen's Gate, wound our way down into the narrow valley of Jehoshaphat, over the south point of Olivet, by the miserable remains of the city of Mary, Martha, and Lazarus, and then prepared ourselves to descend, for you remember that we must go '*down* to Jericho.' And, sure enough, *down*, down we did go, over slippery rocks, for more than a mile when the path became less precipitous. Still, however, the road follows the dry channel of a brook for several miles further, as if descending into the very bowels of the earth. How admirably calculated for 'robbers!' After leaving the brook, which turns aside too far to the south, we ascended and descended naked hills for several miles, the prospect gradually becoming more and more gloomy. Not a house, not even a tree, is to be seen; and the only remains are those of a large *khan*, said to have been the inn to which the good Samaritan brought the wounded Jew. Not far from here, in a narrow defile, an English traveller was attacked, shot, and robbed in 1820. As you approach the plain, the mountains wear a more doleful appearance, the ravines become more frightful, and the narrow passages less and less passable. At length the weary pilgrim reaches the plain by a long, steep declivity. . . ."[3] So it was more than a hundred years ago; and even in our day of automobiles and modern transportation, the road has been the scene of many robberies.

The travelers in the parable were four in number. First, there was the victim. He was doubtless a Jew. One might think that he was a reckless fellow, traveling alone on such a dangerous road; but no particular point is to be made of this because the other travelers also were by themselves. Second, there was the

[1] Josephus, *Jewish War* IV. 8. 3.

[2] Jerome, *On Jeremiah* I. 50.

[3] W. M. Thomson, *The Land and the Book* (London: T. Nelson and Sons, 1883), p. 613.

priest. There were many priests in Palestine. Since the time of David, the priests had been divided into twenty-four courses or orders (see 1 Chronicles 24:1-19). Each order served in the temple twice a year, a week at a time. Jericho like Jerusalem was a city of priests, so priests and Levites often were seen moving to and fro on the desert road. The priest in the story took one look at the wounded man and passed by on the other side. Third, there was a Levite. The Levites were the members of the tribe of Levi who were not priests. They served as assistants to the priests in the many functions of the temple service (see 1 Chronicles 23:24-32). The Levite like the priest, according to the parable, looked at the man and passed by on the other side. Thus the priest and the Levite by their occupations recognized the claims of God, but in their lives they failed to recognize the claims of humanity.

The last man to appear on the scene was a Samaritan. The Jews looked upon the Samaritans as rascals and renegades. The strife between the two groups was of long standing. When the Northern Kingdom was conquered by the Assyrians in 722 B.C., thousands of Israel's leading citizens were deported and were replaced by peoples brought in from Babylon. In time the Israelites who were left in the land intermarried with the foreigners. This made the Samaritans a mixed race, and it was something that the Jews could not forget. More than two centuries later, when the Jews were rebuilding their temple under Zerubbabel, the Samaritans offered their assistance in the work, but their offer was turned down. This blunt refusal by the Jews aggravated the old feelings of envy, with the eventual result that the Samaritans withdrew themselves entirely from the Jews and built their own temple of worship on Mt. Gerizim. In the time of Christ the bitterness between Jew and Samaritan was so great that Jews traveling from Galilee to Jerusalem often would cross over to the east side of the Jordan and come through Perea rather than go through the country of the Samaritans. Yet in the parable it was the renegade Samaritan who became the hero.

Three Pictures of the Christian

It has been said that this parable is the most practical of all the parables. It gets down to the bottom of what Christianity really is. There is no room here for pious platitudes and hairsplitting definitions, no place for Christianity in the abstract or for a religion to be seen of men. With one scene that flashes upon the screen, Jesus compels us to see that *Christianity is a way of living*. In this scene we see three pictures of the Christian at work.

1. *The Christian's compassion.* In the parable the Samaritan differs from the priest and the Levite in many respects, but the first and main difference is that the Samaritan had a compassionate heart. Here was a man who was in trouble and needed help. The priest and the Levite did not know him and so they did not care. The Samaritan did not know him either, but his heart would not let him pass him by. Each act of the Samaritan goes back to a heart of compassion. A story is told of a man in the depression of the 1930's who was begging. He could find no work, he had no one to turn to. One day he walked up to a well-dressed man on the street and said, "Sir, can you spare me a little money for something to eat?" The man began to put him off, making one excuse and then another. Finally, stretching out his arm, the beggar said, "Sir, if you can't let me have the money, would you mind shaking my hand?" What the man needed more than food was understanding and sympathy.

The world does indeed need compassion. It needs scientists and engineers and astronauts; it needs men with new plans and big ideas; but it needs men with big hearts. "Blessed are the merciful" (Matthew 5:7). "Put on then, as God's chosen ones, holy and beloved, compassion, kindness, lowliness, meekness, and patience" (Colossians 3:12). "Be merciful, even as your Father is merciful" (Luke 6:36). The Samaritan had perfect compassion. Often we are like the priest and the Levite. Doubtless the two could have listed a hundred reasons why they did not stop and give aid. We too hesitate and make excuses for not helping others. We say, "Lord, they do not deserve any help." The Lord says in this parable, "The point is not who *deserves* your help but who *needs* your help." We say, "Lord, they have brought it on themselves." And the Lord says, "That may well be true. But you have brought much on yourselves, and still I am merciful." Many an individual looking for help has found only a cold world; and sometimes, as in this parable, the people with the coldest hearts are those who profess the most upright orthodoxy.

2. *The Christian's conduct.* In the parable the Samaritan exemplifies the principles of Christian conduct. All the world remembers his compassion, but this is so because his compassion led to instant action. Compassion is not real if it is no more

than an emotion. Real compassion affects conduct. And that, after all, is what Christianity is about. There are different rules that men go by in their conduct. First, there is the Iron Rule. The Iron Rule says, "Might makes right." The robbers in the parable illustrate this rule. They assembled in a band, armed themselves, and ambushed a lone traveler, robbing him and beating him and leaving him unconscious in the ditch. They put in action the principle announced by Thrasymachus in Plato's *The Republic* that "justice is nothing else than the interest of the stronger."[4] Might and strength was the only law they knew. Their philosophy was, "What is thine is mine, I'll take it." Second, there is the Silver Rule. The Silver Rule states, "Do not to others what you would not have them do to you." The priest and the Levite followed this rule. These two ecclesiastics did not do the wounded man any harm, but neither did they do him any good. Many people are like this. Their religion is purely a negative matter. They feel that being a Christian consists in *not* doing certain things. They have no sense of responsibility for other people. They do not think of others, they do not pray for others. They are content with being left alone, and they leave everybody else alone. Their philosophy is, "What is mine is mine. I'll keep it."

The other rule seen in the story is the Golden Rule. It says, "As you wish that men would do to you, do so to them" (Luke 6:31). This was the rule the Samaritan lived by. When he saw the wounded man, he pictured himself in the ditch, and he knew what he must do. His duty was to help. He stopped and went to the man; he gave him first aid; he put him on his own animal; he led him to the inn; he watched over him through the night; and the next morning, when he had to go on his way, he made sure that the man would be cared for. From beginning to end and through it all he was asking himself the question, "What more can I do?" So the religion of the Golden Rule is positive. It is practical service that counts in Christ's kingdom. Christianity is more than going to Church and saying prayers. A group of people can do these things for years and be a dead church. Christianity is a way of living. It is a way of giving oneself to others. The philosophy of the Christian is, "What is mine is thine. We'll share it."

3. *The Christian's circle.* In the parable the Samaritan shows that the circle of Christian responsibility is the world. The Jews in the time of Christ lived in a narrow, self-centered world. They hated all other people and regarded them as unclean. By

---

[4]Plato, *The Republic* I.

their attitudes and their traditions they erected barriers that made it impossible for them to live peaceably with all men. The law indeed said that one was to love his neighbor, but the Jews had interpreted this command to mean that a Jew was to love only a fellow Jew. They felt no obligation to the Gentiles. They said, for example, if on the Sabbath a wall were to collapse on a man, enough of it could be removed to see if the victim was a Jew or a Gentile. If he was a Jew, he could be helped; if he was a Gentile, nothing could be done for him without violating the Sabbath.[5] It is little wonder, then, that Jesus selected a hated Samaritan to have the leading part in His story. It is easy for us today to find fault with the petty prejudices of the Jews, but the fact remains that most of the people who get *our* help are our friends. To whom do we grant favors? Whom do we invite to dinner? For whom do we pray? We are quick to serve others if they are our companions. We are ready to relieve the afflicted or clothe the orphans, but we first want to inquire if they are of our own group. But the demands of humanity in misery cannot be restricted to social caste or color or creed. We too need to ask, "Who is my neighbor?"

"Go and Do Likewise"

Jesus concluded His story by asking the lawyer which one of the three proved to be neighbor to the man who fell among thieves. The lawyer hedged a bit and then said, "The man who showed mercy." "All right, there's the answer to your question," said Jesus. "You go and do the same thing."

Jesus' story of the Samaritan fixes attention on *my* obligations to all men. I owe others something which I must pay. The question is not so much "Who is my neighbor?" but "Whose neighbor am I?" We are all travelers. And there are only two sides of life's road, this side and the other side. The unnamed Samaritan traveled this side — "the attentive look, the compassionate heart, the helpful hand, the willing foot, the open purse" — and became immortal.

[5]William Barclay, *And Jesus Said: A Handbook on the Parables of Jesus* (Edinburgh: The Church of Scotland Youth Committee, 1952), p. 77. For numerous other illustrations of Jewish attitude toward Gentiles, see Alfred Edersheim, *The Life and Times of Jesus the Messiah*, Vol. I, pp. 90-92. Although this is an old work, it contains in convenient form much valuable information on Jewish laws and customs.

THE FRIEND AT MIDNIGHT

"And he said to them, 'Which of you who has a friend will go to
him at midnight and say to him, "Friend, lend me three loaves; for
a friend of mine has arrived on a journey, and I have nothing to set
before him"; and he will answer from within, "Do not bother me; the
door is now shut, and my children are with me in bed; I cannot
get up and give you anything"? I tell you, though he will not get up
and give him anything because he is his friend, yet because of his
importunity he will rise and give him whatever he needs. And I
tell you, Ask and it will be given you; seek, and you will find; knock,
and it will be opened to you. For every one who asks receives, and he
who seeks finds, and to him who knocks it will be opened. What father
among you, if his son asks for a fish, will instead of a fish give him a
serpent; or if he asks for an egg, will give him a scorpion? If you, then,
who are evil, know how to give good gifts to your children, how much
more will the heavenly Father give the Holy Spirit to those who ask
him?' "

(Luke 11:5-13)

THE PERSISTENT WIDOW

"And he told them a parable, to the effect that they ought always
to pray and not lose heart. He said, 'In a certain city there was a
judge who neither feared God nor regarded man; and there was a
widow in that city who kept coming to him and saying, "Vindicate
me against my adversary." For awhile he refused; but afterward he
said to himself, "Though I neither fear God nor regard man, yet because this widow bothers me, I will vindicate her, or she will wear
me out by her continual coming." ' And the Lord said, 'Hear what
the unrighteous judge says. And will not God vindicate his elect,
who cry to him day and night? Will he delay long over them? I tell
you, he will vindicate them speedily. Nevertheless, when the Son
of man comes, will he find faith on earth?' "

(Luke 18:1-8)

10

PERSISTENCE IN PRAYER

Jesus must have spoken a number of parables on prayer, but these two are the only ones recorded that deal specifically with the subject of prayer. They are both found in the Gospel of Luke. According to Luke the two parables were given on different occasions, but each obviously enforces the lessons of the other.

The Friend at Midnight

The Parable of the Friend at Midnight is a homely story that has a touch of humor in it. A traveler turned in at a house late at night. He was welcomed, but since his arrival was unexpected there was no food to put before him. It was a most embarrassing circumstance, for the hour was late and nothing could be obtained from the market place. So the host hurried out down the street to the house of a friend. He banged on the locked door and cried out to his friend inside, explaining his predicament. But his friend did not want to be bothered. Of course, it is easy to see why he did not want to get up. In Palestine the majority of the people were poor and most of the houses were one-room cottages. The house was built on the ground, with beaten clay serving as the floor. The animals were usually kept inside to protect them against the weather and possible theft. In part of the house a platform was raised above the floor on stilts. It was in this upper story where the family cooked and ate and slept together. Quite naturally, then, the man did not want to get out of bed because it would disturb the whole household. But the desperate host continued to bang on the door outside. Soon it became obvious that if the family was to get any rest at all, there was nothing else to do but to get up, let the man in and give him what he wanted.

The Persistent Widow

The other parable, the Parable of the Persistent Widow, is very similar. There was a widow in a city who was being oppressed. In the same city there was a judge who had no respect for God or man. The judge was probably a Roman, because one man could not constitute a Jewish court. The widow kept coming to the judge and pleading her cause, while he continued giving her a deaf ear. Perhaps the judge, like Felix (see Acts 24:26), was delaying the matter, expecting a bribe. But the woman was penniless, and all she could do was to keep on badgering and pestering the judge until he finally gave in.

Lessons on Prayer

Taken together the twin parables teach us much about prayer. Naturally they do not cover every principle on prayer, yet from these parables certain clear-cut lessons stand out.

1. *Responsibility in prayer.* Jesus taught that prayer is an obligation. The beginning point of the Parable of the Persistent Widow is that men "ought always to pray and not lose heart" (Luke 18:1). Another way to translate this would be to say that men "must" pray. Why did the widow go to the judge again and again? Because she was in urgent need. And why did the man run down the street and wake up his friend at midnight? Because he was in need and he did not know where else he could go. Men *must* pray, for like the widow and the host they stand in need of something which they cannot supply themselves.

Luke preserves the beautiful scene that leads up to the Parable of the Friend at Midnight (Luke 11:1-4). Jesus was praying in a certain place, and one of the disciples came to Him and said, "Lord, teach us to pray like you pray." Prayer was not an unfamiliar thing to them. But when they saw and heard Jesus pray, it was as though they had never heard a prayer before. Whatever it was that Jesus had in His prayers they wanted in theirs.

It is interesting to notice how Luke, who is the only writer to record these two parables on prayer, draws attention to the prayer-life of Jesus. The great occasions of Jesus' earthly ministry were ushered in with prayer. There is the baptism of Jesus. Luke is the only writer who mentions that Jesus was praying when the Holy Spirit descended upon Him (Luke 3:21). It is Luke who tells us that Jesus continued all night in prayer before choosing the twelve apostles (Luke 6:12-13). Again it is Luke who describes the Great Confession at Caesarea Philippi as being accompanied with prayer (Luke 9:18). And Luke is the only writer to point out that Jesus was praying at the time of His glorification on the Mount of Transfiguration (Luke 9:28). The image of Jesus as a praying man was precious to Luke and to the early church. If Jesus needed prayer, if the early church needed to pray, we cannot need less today.

2. *Requirements of prayer.* In the parabolic illustrations of the host and the widow, Jesus gives in capsule form some of the basic requirements or conditions of effective prayer. First, a prayer must be *direct* and *definite.* The host went directly to his friend and the widow went directly to the judge. Each made a personal request. Prayer is personal and individual. It is a meeting of persons in the seclusion of one's closet (Matthew 6:6). It is a confident entrance to the throne of grace (Hebrews 4:16). It is something that is also definite. The request of the host was to the point: "Friend, lend me three loaves." He did not ask for things in general, but he was specific. Our prayers should be just as specific. When we pray we deal too much in generalities. In fact, our prayers are so general that they can be made to fit most any occasion. This is one reason why too often they are mere forms. If we were more specific in prayer, we would not be so apt to rhyme off phrase after phrase which has no meaning to us. Instead of acknowledging that we are a blessed people, we need to list our blessings and thank God for them one by one. In the same way we should detail our sins, absolutely and literally and grievously confessing them to God. We can and must be frank when we speak to God.

Second, a prayer must be *sincere.* In the parables the host and the widow were utterly sincere in their petitions. Prayer, by its very nature, must come from the heart. Possibly this was what astounded the disciples about the prayers of Jesus. His prayers were warm with feeling, they were the expressions of intense desires. Jesus' prayer in Gethsemane was so earnest that "his sweat became like great drops of blood falling down upon the ground" (Luke 22:44). Jesus did not enter into prayer lightly. With Him it was a vibrant experience, a force in His life for good.

There are good reasons why effective prayer depends on true sincerity. What father would feel obligated to give a gift to his son when he knew that to the son it really made no difference whether he received it or not? So God is not impressed when we routinely ask for things that we really do not want. On the other hand, God knows that when we come to Him with a most urgent request, then we will do all that we can to bring about the accomplishment of the prayer. And that is exactly what God wishes, for He cannot answer our prayers apart from our willingness to help. We may pray for the sick and the afflicted and the poor, but what is the prayer worth unless we are willing to help those for whom we pray? We may pray for the salvation of souls over the world, but will God answer the prayer as long as our hands are clasped in idleness? God will not hear unless it is a prayer of faith, and if it is a prayer of faith that demands every effort of cooperation on our part. Unless a prayer is uttered in dead earnestness it is not prayer.

Third, prayer must be *persistent*. This is the main point of the parables. The host, even though it was late at night, battered and beat on the friend's door until finally he got an answer. The woman kept on pestering the judge until at last he did her justice. Thus Jesus says, "Ask, and it will be given you; seek, and you will find; knock, and it will be opened." That is, interpreting the full sense of these verbs, keep on asking, keep on seeking, keep on knocking — and the response is sure to come. It is not that God needs to be begged. The main truth of the parables is, however, that if men can get what they want through shameless begging, certainly a loving heavenly Father will grant the requests of His children.

3. *Rewards of prayer*. In these parables we see that earnest prayer is rewarded. The host did not go away from his friend's door empty handed, nor did the widow continue to suffer abuse from her enemy. Their efforts were favorably rewarded. God always rewards true prayer, and His reward is abundant. This is clearly brought out in the context of the Parable of the Friend at Midnight. The passage reads: "For every one who asks receives, and he who seeks finds, and to him who knocks it will be opened. What father among you, if his son asks for a fish, will instead of a fish give him a serpent; or if he asks for an egg, will give him a scorpion? If you then, who are evil, know how to give good gifts to your children, how much more will the heavenly Father give the Holy Spirit to those who ask him?" The expression "How much more" is very important. The point is this: if men will respond when requests are made of them, *how much more* will God give good things to those who ask Him! (The best gift of all is the Holy Spirit.) These parables teach,

then, that God gives blessing upon blessing to those who make sincere request of Him.

Yet it is quite true that not all prayers are answered. In spite of David's pleading, his little child died (2 Samuel 12:15-24); and notwithstanding Paul's prayer, his "thorn in the flesh" was not taken away (2 Corinthians 12:7-9). The fact is that if God is indeed a wise Father, that as long as He is the Supreme Sovereign of the universe, there will be certain things that we ask for that cannot be granted. Past experience tells us this is so. It is possible that today we are praying for something which is directly opposite to what we asked for a year ago. Not a few times do we find ourselves thanking God because He did not answer some prayer in the past. This happens because we cannot see into the future, we do not understand the past, and we only know a little piece of the present. God alone knows the whole scheme of things. Therefore, the perfect prayer is the outpouring of a strong, intense desire, but with the humble resignation, "Not my will, but Thy will be done."

THE PARABLE OF THE RICH FOOL

"One of the multitude said to him, 'Teacher, bid my brother divide the inheritance with me.' But he said to him, 'Man, who made me a judge or divider over you?' And he said to them, 'Take heed, and beware of all covetousness; for a man's life does not consist in the abundance of his possessions.' And he told them a parable, saying, 'The land of a rich man brought forth plentifully; and he thought to himself, "What shall I do, for I have nowhere to store my crops?" And he said, "I will do this: I will pull down my barns, and build larger ones; and there I will store all my grain and my goods. And I will say to my soul, Soul, you have ample goods laid up for many years; take your ease, eat, drink, and be merry." But God said to him, "Fool! This night your soul is required of you; and the things you have prepared, whose will they be?" So is he who lays up treasure for himself, and is not rich toward God.'"

(Luke 12:13-21)

11

LAYING UP TREASURES FOR SELF

"Provide yourselves with purses that do not grow old, with a treasure in the heavens that does not fail, where no thief approaches and no moth destroys. For where your treasure is, there will your heart be also" (Luke 12:33-34). These words were spoken by Jesus to His "little flock" in the presence of a multitude. They are parallel to His more familiar words given by Matthew in the Sermon on the Mount (Matthew 6:19-21), and they form the conclusion of His special discourse on the subject of material possessions. It is correct to speak of it as a "special discourse," for it probably would not have been delivered to that audience were it not for an unusual incident that took place. This incident provided the occasion for Jesus' story known as the Parable of the Rich Fool.

A Warning against Covetousness

While Jesus was talking with His disciples, a man spoke up and said, "Teacher, tell my brother to divide the inheritance with me." Jesus had been speaking of vital truths, of Divine Providence, of confession and the Holy Spirit, so the man's demand broke into His chain of thought and was entirely out of order. Such an interruption made it obvious that he was not concerned with spiritual things, that his whole heart and life were absorbed with the present age. To this disgruntled individual Jesus said, "Man, who set me over you to judge or arbitrate?" It was a blunt question with a blunt refusal to have anything to do with a quarrel over family property. The Jewish law was specific enough on cases of this kind. The law said that the firstborn son was to receive a double portion (two-thirds) of the inheritance, and that the remainder was to be divided among the other sons (Deuteronomy 21:15-17). This was a law of long standing that allowed no debate. The man who spoke to Jesus obviously was the younger brother. He thought he might be able to get the

Galilean Teacher on his side in order to get an equal share of
the inheritance. He knew the law, but he was covetous and
wanted more than his rightful share.

What follows is the most severe warning in the Bible against
covetousness. "Watch out," said Jesus. "Be on your guard against
all kinds of covetousness." The warning, as is clear in the Greek
text, is against covetousness in any and all forms.[1] But what is
covetousness? It is not simply a desire for property. A simple
illustration may help to answer this question. Here is an individual
who has an excessive, unrestrained desire for food. It can be
said of him that he is "greedy for food." Just as some people
are greedy for food, others are greedy for gain. Theirs is a selfish
ambition to get more and more; they are never satisfied with what
they have. And this is exactly what covetousness is — it is greed
or avarice, an excessive or inordinate desire for gain.

After warning against covetousness, Jesus states the reason for
the warning: "A man's life does not consist in the abundance of
his possessions." This is one rendering of a clause that is very
difficult to translate. The New English Bible puts it another way:
"Even when a man has more than enough, his wealth does not
give him life." Either way it is expressed, Jesus plainly means
that life is more than things, that the success of a man's work
cannot be measured in terms of what he has been able to ac-
cumulate.

The Warning Illustrated

Jesus then tells a story of a rich man to illustrate His meaning.
There was a man who for years had been making a lot of money.
One year he had a bumper crop, and he did not know what
to do with all his grain. He decided that he would solve the
problem by tearing down his already spacious barns and building
larger ones. Then, he thought, no drouth or depression would
be able to touch him; he could lean back and enjoy himself for
years to come. But God told him that very night he was going
to die and thus dashed his plans to pieces forever.

If the Parable of the Good Samaritan is the most practical of
all the parables, the Parable of the Rich Fool is the most necessary.

[1]The Greek adjective *pases* is to be translated *every kind of, all sorts of.*
Thus the New English Bible renders this passage: "Beware! Be on your
guard against greed of every kind. . . ." See William F. Arndt and F. Wilbur
Gingrich, *A Greek-English Lexicon of the New Testament and Other Early
Christian Literature* (Chicago: University of Chicago Press, 1957), p. 636.

Evidences of covetousness are on every hand. While adultery, drunkenness, and dishonesty are still frowned upon, covetousness rides roughshod through modern society and is ignored. Even among professed Christians it is so prevalent that it is scarcely recognized for what it is — a deadly sin. A worldly atmosphere so pervades the church that its very life is threatened. Individual members are in such hot pursuit of their own interests that they have little time and energy left for the Lord. How we need to take the teachings of Jesus to heart! Here was a man who apparently was a great success, yet God called him a fool. What was wrong with his life? How did he miss the way? How did he act like a fool? This man was a fool because of the important things he forgot.

1. *He forgot other people.* The first thing that leaps out from the story is that the man thought of no one except himself. His debate with himself is given in a few words. Six times the pronoun "I" is used, and five times "my" is found. We read sadly, "What shall *I* do, for *I* have nowhere to store *my* crops?" "*I* will do this: *I* will pull down *my* barns . . . and there *I* will store all *my* grain and *my* goods." One gets the distinct impression that these schemes were formulated by self and for self. Other people never entered the man's mind. Not once did he remember those who labored for him in seedtime and at harvest. As he was saying to himself, "What can I do, for I have no place to put my crops?" perhaps a neighbor across his field was saying, "What can I do, for I don't even have bread for my children?" If the rich man did not have enough barns, there were other places where he could have put his grain. As Ambrose expressed it, "Thou *hast* barns, — the bosoms of the needy, — the houses of the widows, — the mouths of orphans and of infants."[2] But the rich man did not think of these barns, for in his little world there was room for no one but himself.

2. *He forgot that a man is more than what he owns.* The rich man conceived of life only in terms of physical things. It is here that he made a tragic mistake: he did not distinguish between *what a man has and what a man is.* To be sure, it is not always easy to make a definite distinction. Many of us who have had the benefit of Christian training still count a man fortunate if he enjoys a long run of prosperity. In contrast the Scriptures say, "How hard it will be for those who have riches to

---

[2]Cited by Richard Chenevix Trench, *Notes on the Parables of Our Lord,* Fourteenth Edition, Revised. (London: Macmillan and Co., 1882), p. 340.

enter the kingdom of God" (Mark 10:23). "But those who desire to be rich fall into temptation, into a snare, into many senseless and hurtful desires that plunge men into ruin and destruction. For the love of money is the root of all evils; it is through this craving that some have wandered away from the faith and pierced their hearts with many pangs" (1 Timothy 6:9-10). "As for the rich in this world, charge them not to be haughty, not to set their hopes on uncertain riches but on God who richly furnishes us with everything to enjoy. They are to do good, to be rich in good deeds, liberal and generous, thus laying up for themselves a good foundation for the future, so that they may take hold of the life which is life indeed" (1 Timothy 6:17-19). The basis of inventory for a man's life is not the same as in his business. So it is more important to be rich in good deeds than to be rich in goods.

3. *He forgot the source of real happiness.* Since the rich man had a false conception of life, he also had a false conception of happiness. He thought that he could be happy by eating and drinking and indulging himself. There was another man, this one from Old Testament times, who made the same futile attempt. He wrote the Book of Ecclesiastes, and in it he tells of his quest for happiness. "I searched with my mind how to cheer my body with wine . . . and how to lay hold on folly, till I might see what was good for the sons of men to do under heaven during the few days of their life. I made great works; I built houses and planted vineyards for myself; I made myself gardens and parks, and planted in them all kinds of fruit trees. I made myself pools from which to water the forest of growing trees. I bought male and female slaves, and had slaves who were born in my house; I had also great possessions of herds and flocks, more than any who had been before me in Jerusalem. I also gathered for myself silver and gold and the treasure of kings and provinces; I got singers, both men and women, and many concubines, man's delight . . . . And whatever my eyes desired I did not keep from them; I kept my heart from no pleasure" (Ecclesiastes 2:3-10). But after he had done all these things and had evaluated their worth, he bent down and wrote on his whirlpool of fortune and fun, "All is vanity and a striving after wind" (verse 11). He came to realize, like countless others long since, that *happiness is not to be found in things.* Money can buy much, but money cannot buy a sense of usefulness, a clear conscience, and a mind content

with God and man. These are the true riches, without which
no man can be really happy.

4. *He forgot God.* The greatest blunder of the rich man was
that he did not take God into account. There was nothing wrong
with his decision to tear down his barns and build larger ones.
A good farmer must have foresight and plan ahead. But his fatal
mistake was that in all of his well-laid plans not one thought
had been given to God. A common downfall of many believers is
to forget God when they are making their plans. Thus James
wrote: "Come now, you who say, 'Today or tomorrow we will go
into such and such a town and spend a year there and trade
and get gain'; whereas you do not know about tomorrow. What
is your life? For you are a mist that appears for a little time
and then vanishes. Instead you ought to say, 'If the Lord wills,
we shall live and we shall do this or that'" (James 4:13-15).
Whatever our long-range plans may be, let us remember that
the biggest factor of all is God. If we leave Him out of our plans,
they are sure to end in ruin.

5. *He forgot death.* The rich man thought that he was going
to live a long life. He made his plans for "many years," yet he
had only one day left. We too deceive ourselves in thinking that
we have plenty of time. We put off till tomorrow, and yet we
do not know if there will be a tomorrow. As someone has put it,
the devil no longer says to man, "You will not die," but rather,
"You will not die *so soon.*" An Arab proverb says, "Death is a
black camel which kneels at the gates of all." The Bible says:

> For all our days pass away under thy wrath,
> Our years come to an end like a sigh.
> The years of our life are threescore and ten,
> Or even by reason of strength fourscore;
> Yet their span is but toil and trouble;
> They are soon gone, and we fly away.
> (Psalms 90:9-10)

In the height of his prosperity and self-satisfaction, God appeared to the rich man and required his life. How much did
he leave? *All that he had.* How foolish that he spent all his
life striving for the things he had to leave behind and neglecting
the true values that he could have taken with him. He had a good
title on earth, but no permanent lease and no title in heaven.
One night his soul slipped out from it all — all his wealth and
ease and self-indulgence — and went as a hungry beggar into the
presence of God. "So is he who lays up treasure for himself,
and is not rich toward God."

THE PARABLE OF THE BARREN FIG TREE

"There were some present at that very time who told him of the Galileans whose blood Pilate had mingled with their sacrifices. And he answered them, 'Do you think that these Galileans were worse sinners than all the other Galileans, because they suffered thus? I tell you, No; but unless you repent you will all likewise perish. Or those eighteen upon whom the tower in Siloam fell and killed them, do you think that they were worse offenders than all the others who dwelt in Jerusalem? I tell you, No; but unless you repent you will all likewise perish.'

"And he told this parable: 'A man had a fig tree planted in his vineyard; and he came seeking fruit on it and found none. And he said to the vinedresser, "Lo, these three years I have come seeking fruit on this fig tree, and I find none. Cut it down; why should it use up the ground?" And he answered him, "Let it alone, sir, this year also, till I dig about it and put on manure. And if it bears fruit next year, well and good; but if not, you can cut it down."' "

(Luke 13:1-9)

12

THE TRAGEDY OF FRUITLESSNESS

This parable is an illustration and expansion of Jesus' teaching
on repentance. It was a common belief in Bible times that sickness and disease and violent death were the direct results of sin,
that if a dreadful calamity struck a man it must be because of
some wicked deed he had done. With this confused conception
of sin, a group of people approached Jesus and told Him about
a disaster that had recently taken place. "There were some
Galileans," they said, "who were worshiping in the temple. While
they were in the very act of offering their sacrifices, Pilate's
brutal soldiers came up and slaughtered them, mixing their blood
with the blood of the slain sacrifices. It was a horrible sight.
What abominable sinners they must have been for such a thing
to happen to them!" "No, you are wrong," said Jesus. "They
were no more worse than the rest. And I tell you unless you
yourselves repent you will perish like they did. Do you think
that the tower in Siloam fell on those eighteen people because
they were despicable sinners? No, they were no worse than
you; therefore, unless you repent you will also perish."

The Parable and Its Immediate Application

Then Jesus told them a story. "There was a man who had
a fig tree. Again and again he came looking for fruit, but he
found none. So he told the vinedresser to cut the tree down
and not let it take up space. But the vinedresser asked permission
to work with it a little longer. If in the next year it did not
bear fruit, then it could be cut down."

The fig tree in ancient Palestine was the most important of all
trees. In a warm climate, like that of Palestine, it was fruitful
during much of the year. In April it began to put out its so-
called "immature figs"; then followed its two main crops, an
early one in June and a later one in August. The fig tree was
valued for other reasons. Although it was not a large tree, ranging

on an average from ten to fifteen feet high, its foliage was re-
markably dense, well-suited for a cool shade from the summer
heat. The fig tree was recognized as a symbol of peace and
prosperity. In the time of Solomon it is said that "Judah and
Israel dwelt in safety, from Dan even to Beer-sheba, every man
under his vine, and under his fig tree" (1 Kings 4:25). Thus
'he fig tree was an invaluable tree and was grown all over the
l\nd of Palestine.

In the parable the fig tree was a cultivated tree. It was planted
in a "vineyard." This may mean that it was planted in some
choice spot among the grapevines in a vineyard, or that it was
planted along with other fig trees in an orchard. The latter
view is in keeping with the custom in Palestine of planting fig
trees and other trees together in groves or orchards. The original
word *ampelon,* translated "vineyard," can refer to an orchard as
well as to a vineyard.

The immediate meaning of the parable is at once apparent
from the context. Jesus had used the murder of the Galileans
and the accident at Siloam as stern warnings to call the Jews
to repentance. He then climaxed His appeal for reform with the
Parable of the Barren Fig Tree. Quite obviously the fig tree
represents the Jewish nation. As the fig tree was planted in a
vineyard, the Jewish nation was nurtured like a favored child
with the blessings of divine revelation and guidance. Throughout
the years of the Old Testament the Lord of Hosts, like the owner
of the vineyard, had come in the hope of finding some evidence
of fruit on the tree. The three years in the parable are not to
be taken literally, but stand for that long period when the Jews
continued in stubborn barrenness. The owner's decree to cut
the tree down symbolizes the impending devastation of Jerusalem
and the destruction of the Jewish nation as a whole. The pleading of the vinedresser for a little more time means that God
would give the rebellious nation yet one more chance, and then
if it did not bear fruit it would be finally and irrevocably cut
down from its privileged place.

Lessons for Us

To the Jews who understood, the parable when first spoken
must have been a severe blow. It was aimed directly at them
and forecast the doom of their race. Yet the basic principles
of the story did not pass away with the Jewish nation, but are

applicable for all time. The lessons for us center around the barren tree and the tolerant owner.

1. *The barren tree.* There are several things that can be said about this barren tree. The first is that it was useless. Because it had no fruit, it was absolutely worthless to the owner. It was of no use. This is an apt description of many people in the church today. The painful truth is that a large number of professed Christians are totally useless. They are not wicked, they are not lawbreakers. They are neither violent nor revengeful nor hateful. They simply are of no use. And this in the eyes of Jesus is the greatest of failures. He declared that to be His followers was to be like the salt of the earth (Matthew 5:13). That was His way of saying that Christians by their very nature must be supremely useful. What could unsalty salt be used for? It was good for nothing except to be thrown out on the roadways of Palestine for people to walk on. Other parables of Jesus underscore His teachings on the sin of uselessness. There are the parables of Judgment recorded in Matthew 25. In each of these parables the individual is cast out into the night of condemnation not because of something wrong he had done but because of something right he had left undone. The five virgins were foolish because they did not bring with them enough oil. The one-talent man was accounted wicked solely because he did not use what he had. Those on the left hand had to depart not due to any special immorality, but because they had neglected to give bread and water and clothing to the distressed. So the true test of what a man is worth is a very simple one: To what use is he putting his life? What is he worth to God and man? God measures worth in terms of use. He does not demand the impossible or the sensational or the extraordinary, but He does expect from every tree *some* fruit. The Roman writer Phaedrus said, "Unless what we do is useful, our glory is vain."[1]

Second, the fig tree not only was useless, but it was hindering good from being done. "Why should it use up the ground?" was the question of the owner. The fig tree was in the way. It was guilty of taking in nourishment from the soil without giving anything in return. Too many people in the church are like that. Instead of being useful, they waste space. Like the fruitless fig tree, they do not bear fruit themselves and they get in the way of the others that do. For example, here is a person who has put on Christ in baptism. He claims to be a member of the body

[1]Phaedrus, *Fables* III. 17.12.

of Christ. Yet he seldom attends the worship services of the
church, gives only a few pennies to its support, and never actively
cooperates in the program of work it has undertaken to do.
Not only so, but he is a perpetual critic and faultfinder. To hear
him tell it, nothing is ever done right or run right. He says
that he is a church member, but his life is as uninviting as a
desert. His life is sterile and vain, and he is a nuisance to the
church. The greatest crime against humanity is for one to be a
parasite on society, for one to be always taking out of the world
more than he puts in. That is the unavoidable consequence of
the tree that does not produce fruit.

Third, the tree being fruitless invited destruction. "Cut it down,"
was the owner's instructions. It was taking up space and had to
be removed. "Every tree that does not bear good fruit is cut
down and thrown into the fire" (Matthew 7:19). "If a man
does not abide in me, he is cast forth as a branch and withers;
and the branches are gathered, thrown into the fire and burned"
(John 15:6). It is a law of nature that whatever does not repro-
duce itself must die. It is a universal law, whether applied to a
tree, a bird, or a man. A family or church takes its own life if
it is not self-perpetuating. Whose fault was it that the fig tree
in the parable had to be removed? It was not the fault of the
soil or the sunshine or the rain; it was not the fault of the vinedresser or the owner. The truth is that the tree *condemned
itself* by failing to do the work of a tree. Although it was planted
in a protected vineyard, nevertheless it yielded no fruit. And
that is precisely the danger that threatens many of us. We share
in the culture of an advanced age. We live in homes where a
Bible is in almost every room. Yet numbers of us bear no real
fruit. It is not an angry God that condemns us to eternal punishment. We condemn ourselves. So every man that does not find
his place in the world, that never responds to the higher claims
of life on him, at the end in Judgment will stand self-condemned.
Fruitlessness invites disaster.

2. *The tolerant owner.* The other grand truth of the parable
is brought out in the lingering patience of the owner. "Lo, these
three years I have come seeking fruit," he says in disappointment.
More than three annual visits are implied. Since the fig tree
yielded several crops in the year, it is not unreasonable to assume
that the owner came time and again, month after month — early
spring, early summer and late summer — and still the tree was
fruitless. The God of all creation is likewise patient with us.

How many times has He come expecting to find some sign of fruit in our lives, and turned away in utter disappointment! He waits, and then returns for another visit. He is disappointed again, but still He continues in understanding and forbearance. He delays even more. He is slow to anger and long-suffering with us. If He were not, what would become of us? If He did not delay in judgment, not one soul would escape condemnation. But He has delayed in passing judgment, and He is delaying, "not wishing that any should perish, but that all should reach repentance" (2 Peter 3:9).

Yet even Divine patience can be exhausted. God waits long, but the Scriptures solemnly warn that there is a limit to His waiting. In the parable a definite period of grace was given to the fig tree. One more year was to be allowed, and no more. There is a limit to God's patience and grace. And the Jews had just about reached that limit. The prophets had come and had been rejected. John the Baptist came and preached the urgency of repentance, but most of his hearers remained the same. The Son of God Himself came. His message, and that of His apostles, was to be the final word from heaven to get the Jews to repent. It was their last chance. God could do no more. To reject God's Son and the Holy Spirit was a final rejection which meant the final destruction of the Jewish nation.

The story of the fig tree and the inevitable punishment that the Jewish nation brought on itself forewarn us of the tragedy of fruitlessness. The one escape from this tragedy is contained in the words of Jesus: "Unless you repent you will all likewise perish."

THE PARABLE OF THE WISE AND FOOLISH BUILDERS

" 'Every one then who hears these words of mine and does them will be like a wise man who built his house upon the rock; and the rain fell, and the floods came, and the winds blew and beat upon that house, but it did not fall, because it had been founded on the rock. And every one who hears these words of mine and does not do them will be like a foolish man who built his house upon the sand; and the rain fell, and the floods came, and the winds blew and beat against that house, and it fell; and great was the fall of it.' "

(Matthew 7:24-27)

" 'Why do you call me "Lord, Lord," and not do what I tell you? Every one who comes to me and hears my words and does them, I will show you what he is like: he is like a man building a house, who dug deep, and laid the foundation upon rock; and when a flood arose, the stream broke against that house, and could not shake it, because it had been well built. But he who hears and does not do them is like a man who built a house on the ground without a foundation; against which the stream broke, and immediately it fell, and the ruin of that house was great.' "

(Luke 6:46-49)

13

HEARING AND DOING

In the last section of the Sermon on the Mount, Jesus uses three sets of contrasts to demonstrate the absolute necessity of obedience. The first contrast is that of two ways: one is wide and easy that ends in certain death, and the other is narrow and hard that leads to life. The second contrast is that of two trees, one is good and one is bad. The bad tree cannot produce good fruit and the good tree cannot produce corrupt fruit. Only by their fruits can the two trees be distinguished. Jesus means that the final evaluation of a person's life is determined by his deeds. It is not what a man professes that counts, but what a man *does*. The third contrast, that of the two builders, makes this especially clear.

The Two Accounts

The story of the wise and foolish builders is recorded in both Matthew and Luke. There are slight differences in the two accounts, but basically the story is the same. In Luke one builder digs down deep and sets his foundation on the rock, while the other builder puts his house on the thin soil without thought for the foundation. In this account the actions of the two builders were perfectly normal, the kind of thing that might happen anywhere. In Matthew, however, the story represents what might take place especially in the region of the Bible world. In Palestine there were numerous low valleys and gullies that had been excavated by running water. In the summer these low spots naturally were dry, and often were pleasant and inviting in appearance. But when the rains began in the fall, these gorges became raging torrents which washed away anything in their paths. Perhaps this was the kind of site selected by one builder in the parable. Finding a strand of smooth and level sand, he began to build without thinking a moment about the disaster that his careless actions would surely bring upon him.

Not long afterward, the rains began; the floods mounted and swept his house down the stream in violent destruction. But the other man knew better. Building a house was an important matter to him. He prepared and planned and investigated. He would not make a tragic mistake about his foundation. He searched about until he found solid rock on which he could erect his house and rest secure against the threats of the winter storms. So one builder was wise and the other was foolish. It is rather ridiculous to think that a man would build his house on a sandy river bed, but the absurd folly of such action is the very point of the parable.

A Lesson on Obedience

The Parable of the Wise and Foolish Builders is the strongest lesson that Jesus gave on obedience. "Every one who hears these words of mine and does them" — these are words that ring through the centuries. They are not ordinary words. They are not the words of a preacher, a teacher, or even a prophet. They are much more. They express the stupendous claim of Jesus to be the only guide for men's souls. Jesus laid it down as a positive and inescapable law that all men had to obey Him. Men must listen to Him and keep His words, or else their lives will crumble in defeat.

The verses that lead up to the story of the two builders are emphatic in requiring obedience. According to Matthew, Jesus says: "Not every one who says to me, 'Lord, Lord,' shall enter the kingdom of heaven, but he who does the will of my Father who is in heaven. On that day many will say to me, 'Lord, Lord, did we not prophesy in your name, and cast out demons in your name, and do many mighty works in your name?' And then will I declare to them, 'I never knew you; depart from me, you evildoers'" (Matthew 7:21-23). In Luke the parable is introduced with one question: "Why do you call me 'Lord, Lord,' and not do what I tell you?"(Luke 6:46). Other sayings of Jesus exhibit the same imperative. "My mother and my brothers are those who hear the word of God and do it" (Luke 8:21). "If you know these things, blessed are you if you do them" (John 13:17). "You are my friends if you do what I command you" (John 15:14).

Although we readily consent to these great sayings, still we forget. Too often we find that we are exactly like the man who heard and did not do. Not that there is anything wrong with hearing. It is a wonderful experience, of course, to delight in listening to the Word of God, to grasp with joy every word as it is read and proclaimed. Such a hearer is awakened out of his dull complacency and is transported to a higher realm of life. The Word of God pierces his conscience and he resolves to live a better life. God touches his life through the Word as it is preached, and he receives a blessing. But his blessing may turn into his condemnation, if he fails to put into action the lessons he has gained.

Why We Do Not Obey

The danger of hearing without doing is very real to all of us. It is not that we have never heard the truth. We hear it time and time again, but still we fail to act. Why is it that we do not turn words into actions? How is it that we can hear and not obey? One main reason why we fail to practice what we hear is that *we do not act at once.* We may thoroughly enjoy the Sunday morning sermon and leave the place of worship with a firm intention to do those things that we have neglected to do. But Sunday afternoon is a time for rest, and Monday is a day of work; so by the time Monday evening comes around, that firm intention to act has faded from view and we lapse back into the routine of another unproductive week. We hear the sermon next Sunday morning, but during the week we neglect to keep it. And so it goes, until the more we hear the less we do, until our much hearing and our little doing make it practically impossible that we be worth anything to the kingdom of Christ. So when we are reminded of something that we have neglected to do, or when we look about us and see that there is one particular thing that needs to be done, we should do it right there and at that very moment. Tomorrow will probably be too late. It is not simply that there may be no tomorrow, which may very well be true; but more important, the desire to help others may not be there tomorrow. Emotions need to be expressed; and our inner urgings to do good must be translated into action or else we will do great harm to ourselves. And the plain truth is that unless we do a thing at once, the chances are very great that the thing will not be done at all.

Another reason why our hearing is not turned to action is that *we do not want to be inconvenienced.* In Luke the foolish builder was the man who built his house on the ground surface and did not dig deep for a sure footing. He did not bother about the extra expense and time necessary for a solid foundation. He took the easy way out. Many of us are like that. We do not want to take the trouble that goes with following Christ all the way. We are willing to obey Christ as long as it is pleasant and convenient. Like giving someone a ride, we do not mind carrying the person since we are already going that way. Likewise, we do not mind going along with God's will if we are already going that way. But if His will is in conflict with our own will, then we are ready to part company with Him and go our separate ways. We forget that Christ's mission to earth was not to make it easy for man but to save man. The Christian way is a way of duty, and duty is not always easy. Thus the straightest course to heaven often demands that we go out of the way to lend a hand to somebody else. Is it possible that souls will be kept out of heaven because we did not want to be inconvenienced?

Still another reason why we fail to obey Christ is that *we do not look ahead.* The man who built his house on the bright sand never once thought what a precarious site that would be when the autumn rains began. He had no eye for the future. He did not think ahead, he did not consider the final outcome of his actions. It is necessary in life to take the long view of things. A man who lives only for the present moment will never reach success. The athlete who breaks all of his training rules in quest of momentary pleasures cannot hope to win the big race. He must harden himself by maintaining a rigorous and strict physical schedule. He chooses what is tough and difficult at the moment in order to gain the victory in the end. The student who sports and plays through the weeks of the semester may enjoy himself for awhile, but that joy is short-lived when the time for the final examination arrives and no preparation has been made. The world is full of people who wish that years ago they had taken the long view on education, who, seeking the pleasures of the moment, quit school and tied themselves down to a job with no guarantee for the future. So the choice must be made between what is delightful for the present and what will give delight over the long run. It is no different in following Christ. Either we choose what is pleasurable for the moment and incur disaster later on, or we choose what will prove best when we stand before Him to render accounts.

The Time of Testing

The parable of the two builders makes it clear that the time of testing will come. The favorable, sunny weather will not always last. Jesus' language in the story is very descriptive and forceful. The rains beat down on the roof of the house; the winds attacked its walls; and the floods swirled at its base. The same language is used to describe the storms that struck each house. The time of testing, then, will come to all men, to the good and to the bad; and every house will be tested alike. It is true in this life, for no one is exempt from temptations, burdens, and sorrows. It is true of the life to come. "For we must all appear before the judgment seat of Christ, so that each one may receive good or evil, according to what he has done in the body" (2 Corinthians 5:10).

It is absurd to think that a man would ruin himself by building on the sand. But men do absurd things in religion that they would never dream of doing in ordinary life. After the storm was over, when the man stood there alone with the shambles of his broken house about him, he knew exactly where he had made his mistake. He had neglected the most important matter, his foundation. He built a great house, but great was its fall! So Jesus teaches us in this story what happens to those who are careless and slipshod, who live just any old way. Each man's life is like a house that must be built with care and purpose. Above all, it is the sensible duty of every man to examine the ground on which he is building. He builds in vain unless he hears the words of Jesus and does them.

THE PARABLE OF THE CHIEF SEATS

"Now he told a parable to those who were invited, when he marked how they chose the places of honor, saying to them, 'When you are invited by any one to a marriage feast, do not sit down in a place of honor, lest a more eminent man than you be invited by him; and he who invited you both will come and say to you, "Give place to this man," and then you will begin with shame to take the lowest place. But when you are invited, go and sit in the lowest place, so that when your host comes he may say to you, "Friend, go up higher"; then you will be honored in the presence of all who sit at table with you. For every one who exalts himself will be humbled, and he who humbles himself will be exalted.' "

(Luke 14:7-11)

14

HE WHO HUMBLES HIMSELF

This parable is a bit of Jesus' table-talk as He ate in the house of a distinguished Pharisee. It was a sabbath meal, and from the beginning the Pharisees had been watching to see what He would do. So He astounded them by healing a man on the sabbath. "Is it not lawful to do good on the sabbath?" He had reasoned.

Long ago, customs observed at dinners were quite different from ours today. It is well-known that the ancients of Greek and Roman times ate their meals in reclining positions on low couches drawn up against low tables. Ordinarily the tables were U-shaped, which allowed the servants to serve food about the table with ease. At the head of the table was placed the honored guest, in Jewish circles this honor always being reserved for the rabbis. On his right and left were placed the next most honored guests, and the others were seated around the table in descending order of importance. Quite often the exact hour of the meal was not announced. Some guests would arrive early, others would come late. In Jesus' day many of the Pharisees, especially those of the more prominent sort, would time their arrival so they could make an auspicious entrance and in the presence of all receive the chief seats.

At this particular feast which Jesus attended on the sabbath, the Pharisees were scrutinizing His every move. They were watching Him, and He was watching them. He noticed how they came in, slyly maneuvering around the table for the places of honor. So He spoke to them a parable that was a rebuke of their table manners and a warning on their unsafe spiritual condition. "When you are invited to a feast," He said, "don't pick out the best seats. If you do, suppose someone who is a real dignitary comes in. The host will have to ask you to relinquish your seat, and you will be embarrassed to have to go to the foot of the table. If, on the other hand, you at first take a lower seat, the host will urge you to come up higher, and you will be elevated in the sight of all."

This piece of advice that Jesus gave the Pharisees is called a "parable." It is not a parable that tells a story, but it is still a parable because the lesson is to be interpreted figuratively. It is a parable in the true sense of the word, a comparison that teaches on right relationships in the kingdom of God.

The Principle of Humility

The concluding statement of the parable is, "Every one who exalts himself will be humbled, and he who humbles himself will be exalted" (Luke 14:11). It was a favorite saying of Jesus, a point He often emphasized (see Matthew 23:12; Luke 18:14). It was a truth often remembered in the early church. It was taught by Paul and James and Peter. "Do nothing from selfishness or conceit, but in humility count others better than yourselves. Let each of you look not only to his own interests, but also to the interests of others (Philippians 2:3-4). "Humble yourselves before the Lord and he will exalt you" (James 4:10). "Clothe yourselves, all of you, with humility toward one another, for 'God opposes the proud, but gives grace to the humble.' Humble yourselves therefore under the mighty hand of God, that in due time he may exalt you" (1 Peter 5:5-6). It stands as a basic law in the Messiah's kingdom that the only way for men to go up is for them to go down.

The Pathway to Humility

The principle of humility is obvious and clear. But it is not always easy to find the path that leads to humility. How do we begin? Where is the starting-point of true humility? The place to begin is with oneself. Away from the whirl and rush of things, in quiet, uninterrupted solitude, each person needs to submit to the rigor of self-evaluation. And in the lives of all of us there is much that should keep us humble.

1. *Our physical and bodily weaknesses should keep us humble.* Physically speaking, man is dust.

> As a father pities his children,
>   so the Lord pities those who fear him.
> For he knows our frame;
>   he remembers that we are dust.
> As for man, his days are like grass;
>   he flourishes like a flower of the field;
> for the wind passes over it, and it is gone,
>   and its place knows it no more.
>
> (Psalms 103:13-16)

A man can be an architect or an astronomer, a soldier or a states-
man, but no man is as mighty as he would like to be. There are
trails where man cannot go, cliffs and mountains that he cannot
scale, and galaxies in space which he cannot subdue. Besides this,
man lives his days in the midst of suffering and tears. He does not
know how to ward off pain. He is unable to defend himself against
disease. He cannot disguise the inevitable marks of old age. He
cannot bribe away death. The imminence of death alone is sufficient to keep men humble. That an individual's delicate apparatus
can get so quickly out of balance, that his bodily systems can be so
easily disturbed, that his house of clay can be so swiftly swept away
— all of these things show how insecure life is and when remembered will dash to pieces our selfish pride.

2. *Our mental limitations should keep us humble.* For centuries
man has been accumulating facts and perfecting methods. If all of
this knowledge could be put together in one storehouse, it would
still be infinitesimally small as compared with what man does not
know. Advancements in technology and scientific break-throughs
come painfully slow. No one is more keenly aware of this than the
scholar. The real scholar is perpetually shamed by his ignorance.
In all the history of the world there has not been a truly wise man
who was impressed with his wisdom. The learned Socrates was by
no means the best-loved citizen of ancient Athens. He had a heartless way about him that delighted in humiliating other people. His
favorite pastime was to go through the streets of the city looking for
a wise man. When he found a likely candidate, he would corner him, drill him with a series of unanswerable questions, and
then leave him in the oblivion of his ignorance. If Socrates was
the wisest man in Athens, it was only for the reason, he said, that
he alone knew that he knew nothing at all. Will Rogers put it like
this: "We are all ignorant; we're just ignorant of different things."
A man may be able to speak ten languages and be wholly unable to
keep up his bank balance. A man may be an international authority on the literary classics and not be able to drive a car. A man
may be an expert on machines and all sorts of electrical devices,
and scarcely be able to spell a three-syllable word. The simple
truth is that life has grown to such proportions that no one is able
to be a master of all the arts and a master of all the sciences. The
littleness of our knowledge ought to keep us forever humble.

3. *Our moral weaknesses and failures should keep us humble.*
Carlyle once said: "It is in general more profitable to reckon up

our defeats than to boast of our attainments."[1] Nowhere are defects more obvious to us than in our moral conduct. The purest and noblest of men are ever conscious of sin. The Apostle Paul is an outstanding example of this. At work in his life was a destructive force of self-contradiction. At times he did not do what he wanted, but he did the very things that he hated. "So," he said, "I find it to be a law that when I want to do right, evil lies close at hand. . . . Wretched man that I am! Who will deliver me from the body of this death?" (Romans 7:21, 24). The same apostle speaks of himself as the chiefest of sinners (1 Timothy 1:15). Francis of Assisi, who spent his life in service of the poor, points to himself and says: "Nowhere is there a more wretched, a more miserable, a poorer creature than I." Honest self-examination will bring us face to face with ourselves so that we can see how little we really are. How many of us would be willing right now to meet God in judgment on the terms of our innate goodness and on the basis of the works which we have done in His name? The sum total of our kindness, of our generosity and of our good deeds is deplorably small. This above all things, the mediocre goodness that is in the best of us, should make us conscious of the necessity of humility.

The Pattern of Humility

When a man meets Jesus Christ, and puts his life beside that Life, the marked difference brings guilt and grief. On that last night, within the shadow of the cross, a quarrel arose among His disciples as to which of them was the greatest (Luke 22:24-27). We do not know how the argument began. But since Jesus had gathered with His group to eat the Passover meal, the most important Jewish observance of the year, it is quite likely that the strife was over the seating arrangements around the table. What a poignant tragedy that Jesus in these last hours had to witness His own disciples, like the Pharisees, scrambling for seats of distinction. To put an end to the dispute, Jesus asked: "Which is the greater, one who sits at table, or one who serves? Is it not the one who sits at table? But I am among you as one who serves" (verse 27). Then Jesus arose from His place, stripped off His garments, girded Himself with a towel, as a slave would do, and one by one washed His disciples' feet (John 13:3ff.). They sat there dumbfounded, utterly disgraced, not believing that they could have acted so selfishly. It was scarcely necessary that Jesus remind them to do as He

---

[1]Carlyle, "Signs of the Times," *Essays.*

had done. The Prince of Glory bathing their feet! It was a lesson of love and service that they could not forget.

People in the day of Christ did not believe that a man who pushes himself will be abased, nor that a man who lowers himself will in the end be victorious. And few people believe it today. But Jesus taught the contrary, and what He taught He practiced. When He came into the world He slept in a manger, and when He died He reclined on a cross. Neither at His birth nor at His death could He find a more lowly place. The contrast of His life with our lives is to our shame.

THE PARABLE OF THE GREAT SUPPER

"When one of those who sat at table with him heard this, he said to him, 'Blessed is he who shall eat bread in the kingdom of God!' But he said to him, 'A man once gave a great banquet, and invited many; and at the time for the banquet he sent his servant to say to those who had been invited, "Come; for all is now ready." But they all alike began to make excuses. The first said to him, "I have bought a field, and I must go out and see it; I pray you, have me excused." And another said, "I have bought five yoke of oxen, and I go to examine them; I pray you, have me excused." And another said, "I have married a wife, and therefore I cannot come." So the servant came and reported this to his master. Then the householder in anger said to his servant, "Go out quickly to the streets and lanes of the city, and bring in the poor and maimed and blind and lame." And the servant said, "Sir, what you commanded has been done, and still there is room." And the master said to the servant, "Go out to the highways and hedges, and compel people to come in, that my house may be filled. For, I tell you, none of those men who were invited shall taste my banquet."'"

(Luke 14:15-24)

THE PARABLES OF THE MARRIAGE OF THE KING'S SON AND THE WEDDING GARMENT

"And again Jesus spoke to them in parables, saying, 'The kingdom of heaven may be compared to a king who gave a marriage feast for his son, and sent his servants to call those who were invited to the marriage feast; but they would not come. Again he sent other servants, saying, "Tell those who are invited, Behold, I have made ready my dinner, my oxen and my calves are killed, and everything is ready; come to the marriage feast." But they made light of it and went off, one to his farm, another to his business, while the rest seized his servants, treated them shamefully, and killed them. The king was angry, and he sent his troops and destroyed those murderers and burned their city. Then he said to his servants, "The wedding is ready, but those invited were not worthy. Go therefore to the thoroughfares, and invite to the marriage feast as many as you find." And those servants went out into the streets and gathered all whom they found, both bad and good; so the wedding hall was filled with guests.

" 'But when the king came in to look at the guests, he saw there a man who had no wedding garment; and he said to him, "Friend how did you get in here without a wedding garment?" And he was speechless. Then the king said to the attendants, "Bind him hand and foot, and cast him into the outer darkness; there men will weep and gnash their teeth." For many are called, but few are chosen.'"

(Matthew 22:1-14)

15

THE BANQUET OF THE KINGDOM

The one great quality that dominated the life of Jesus was unselfishness. While He was dining in the presence of the Pharisees, Jesus' thoughts turned to the many people who were not invited. So He spoke to His host in the plainest of terms and said: "When you give a dinner or a banquet, do not invite your friends or your brothers or your kinsmen or rich neighbors, lest they also invite you in return, and you be repaid. But when you give a feast, invite the poor, the maimed, the lame, the blind, and you will be blessed, because they cannot repay you. You will be repaid at the resurrection of the just." These were hard words, they were condemning words. His host must have glared at Him with eyes of censure and anger. But Jesus, with no further word of explanation, stood His ground. Then, in an effort to break the spell and dismiss the question, one of the guests exclaimed: "Blessed is he who shall eat bread in the kingdom of God." Jesus responded with a parable that compares His kingdom to a banquet furnished by God.

The Parable of the Great Supper

Once a man gave a great banquet. First, in keeping with Oriental customs, a general announcement was sent out to inform everybody of the coming event. The date was specified, but the exact hour was not. On the stated day, when all the preparations had been made and everything was in order, the man sent out his servant to tell his invited friends that the hour had arrived for the supper. But each man, for one reason or another, began to beg off and would not come. The servant returned and reported this to his master. The master burned with anger. If his friends were not going to come, they should have declined at the first invitation and not have waited until the last moment. What was to be done? "Go into town," said the master, "and bring in the bystanders, the poor, the crippled, and the neglected, and let them fill the empty places."

The servant obeyed, but still there was room left. "Then hurry out and get those in the country," the master demanded: "for I want the house filled with guests to eat my supper."

A Similar Parable

Matthew records a similar parable (see Matthew 22:1-14), so much like this one that interpreters have maintained that they are but two variations of one original story. But the details of the parables, and their backgrounds, are quite different. The one in Matthew follows in close succession the Parable of the Wicked Husbandmen and sounds a warning note to the Jews who would reject their Messiah. The parable in Luke, however, is not as severe in tone, yet it stands as a warning to all men that they should not take the kingdom for granted. The two parables, then, are independent of each other. Their obvious similarities are due to their common source of origin, the Galilean Teacher.

The Divine Banquet

The first truth that strikes us here is that Jesus compared His kingdom to a sumptuous banquet. It is significant that most of Luke 14 (verses 1-25) has to do with feasts and banquets. In this atmosphere Jesus relates a story to show that entering God's kingdom is like coming to a feast. It was the common belief at that time that when the Messiah came, in the golden age of His reign, all of the Jews would be invited in to sit down at the Messiah's table. Jesus made use of this popular notion and taught that the kingdom is like a banquet. The kingdom is not like a long, dreary funeral procession. It is a festive occasion of warm fellowship and unheard of delight. Each follower of Christ in the kingdom, of course, must bear his own burden, each must carry his own cross. But Christ makes it clear that He did not come to darken an already gloomy world. His mission was to bring "the good news" of the kingdom of God.

Since that time, however, this message of Christ has been distorted beyond the point of recognition. Multitudes have come to believe that one cannot enjoy himself if he is a Christian, that to be a Christian is to denounce every joy and pleasure that abound in a beautiful world. Much of this misconception of Christianity arises out of a distorted view of Jesus. The man from Nazareth was indeed the fulfillment of the Old Testament "man of sorrows," the divine servant who "was wounded for our transgressions" and "bruised for our iniquities" (Isaiah 53:3-5). But this picture of Jesus as the Suffering Servant has been magnified out of proportion. An example of this is a spurious letter written by a certain Publius Lentulus, a supposed contemporary of Pilate. The letter, which was written in Latin and was composed no earlier than the fourth century A.D., purports to give an actual physical description of Jesus. It reads in part: "In reproof and rebuke he is formidable; in exhortation and teaching, gentle and amiable. He has never been seen to laugh, but oftentimes to weep. His person is tall and erect; his hands and limbs beautiful and straight. In speaking he is deliberate and grave, and little given to loquacity. In beauty he surpasses the children of men."[1] So goes the imaginary description. Yet because it was the first written description of Jesus, it had a lasting effect on the art and sculpture of succeeding ages, so that even today Jesus is often pictured as the man who never laughed. But this is not a picture of Jesus at all. The Jesus of the Gospels was real, of flesh and bone, as human as He was divine. He was not an ascetic. He was not a recluse (see Matthew 11:18-19). He could not have been the companion of children, and the friend of tax-collectors if He was a man who never laughed. On the contrary, some of His expressions, such as a man with a board in his eye (Matthew 7:3-5), indicate that He had a rich sense of humor; and His many parabolic illustrations show that He could enjoy a story as much as any man.

If Jesus lived in a way as to enjoy life, His disciples should do the same. They are not expected, in monk fashion, to withdraw from the world and heap punishments and miseries upon their bodies. Nor are they to be bound, like some of the Puritans of the past, by a code so strict that even toys for children are condemned as "the works of the flesh." John Wesley was a great man, but he made some tragic mistakes concerning children. In the year of 1748, he established a school known as the Kingswood School. The children in the school were required to get up at 4:00 A.M., winter and summer. There were no recess periods, no holidays, and no play of any sort on any day.[2] In contrast to this austerity, Jesus said that His kingdom is a kingdom of joy. It is not a joy of bodily dissipation and sensuous living; rather it is a spiritual and eternal and heavenly joy. The joys of God's favor, the redemption

---

[1] As cited by Philip Schaff, *History of the Christian Church,* I, 168-69.

[2] Robert Southey, *The Life of John Wesley* (New York: Frederick A. Stokes Co., 1903), pp. 225-26.

from sin, the comfort of the Holy Spirit, the fellowship of the saints, and the peace of God that surpasses understanding — these are some of the joys of the Christian that make each day like a feast day.

The Frivolous Excuses

When the preparations had been made for the banquet, and the servant went out to announce its exact hour, the invited guests "all alike began to make excuses." The word "alike" is a translation of an obscure Greek expression *apo mias*. It is usually taken to mean "alike" or "unanimously": thus one and all, as if by previous design, began to decline the invitation. There is a possibility, however, as evidenced by recent information from the papyri discoveries, that the expression *apo mias* means "at once": thus all, without the blink of an eye, *immediately* began to excuse themselves.[3] Understood either way, it is plain that those invited simply did not want to come.

The excuses that were offered by the intended guests teach certain lessons. The three excuses may be divided into two classes: the first two have to do with *earthly possessions* and the third concerns *earthly ties*.

1. *Earthly possessions.* The first man said, "I have bought a field, and I must go out and see it." The second man said, "I have bought five yoke of oxen, and I go to examine them." There is little difference between the excuses. Both men were absorbed in their own interests; both were so tied up in their business affairs that they had time for nothing else. They had too much to do. They could not come. Many people are like that today. The life that now is gets their first attention. Their business is their Bible and "making a living" is their creed. They never seem to have time for other people, and, of course, they never have time to worship or pray or think about the future life. Surely this is one reason why God in His wisdom has provided Christians with a special occasion and a special service of worship on the Lord's Day. That day is a special call to put aside the concerns of the week and give attention to the concerns of God. In the assembly brother meets with brother; each encourages the other not to stumble; and each as he reflects on the sacrifice of Christ is reminded once again of the cost of sin. We are exhorted, therefore, not to forsake the worship assembly (Hebrews 10:25). It is not possible for man to live by

---

[3]See Arndt-Gingrich, *A Greek-English Lexicon of the New Testament and Other Early Christian Literature,* p. 88.

bread alone (Matthew 4:4). So we must be sure that the demands of business and earthly possessions do not usurp the demands of God.

2. *Earthly ties.* The third man said, "I have married a wife, and therefore I cannot come." One of the beautiful laws of the Old Testament made allowances for a newly-married man: "When a man is newly married, he shall not go out with the army or be charged with any business; he shall be free at home one year, to be happy with his wife whom he has taken" (Deuteronomy 24:5). Perhaps on the basis of this law the man refused to come. At any rate he felt that he had a perfectly good excuse. He placed the obligations of his family and of his home first, and he expected that everybody would understand.

It is a paradox that something as lovely and sweet as home can stand between a man and his God. Scripture indeed says, "Therefore a man leaves his father and his mother and cleaves to his wife, and they become one flesh" (Genesis 2:24). But to leave father and mother does not mean that one should leave his Father in heaven. Our homes, of course, are among our greatest blessings. But many a great blessing has turned into disaster. There are at least two ways in which we can use our homes wrongfully. First, our home and family ties can occupy the chief spot in our hearts. The excuse of the man who could not leave his wife should be compared with Jesus' statement a few verses later: "If any one comes to me and does not hate his own father and mother and wife and children and brothers and sisters, yes, and even his own life, he cannot be my disciple" (Luke 14:26). Jesus demands an exclusive affection. He wants the whole heart, brother or mother or wife not excepted. Second, our homes can be used selfishly. We can come home after work each day and want to do nothing but relax and enjoy ourselves. Or we can spend so much time and effort making our homes livable that we wrap ourselves up in luxury and shut others out. However our homes are built, the windows should always look out on the needs of others. Hospitality was a great virtue in New Testament times (Romans 12:13; Hebrews 13:2); and hospitality remains today the great glory of a Christian home.

The Universal Invitation

The flimsy excuses made the host angry: those especially invited did not want to come. So he sent his servant out into the city to bring in the poor and the maimed and blind and lame.

They were gathered from the "streets and lanes" of the town, the public places where those who had no comfortable homes were likely to be found. Still there was room. "Then, go out of the city to the highways and hedgerows," said the host. "I want my house to be full." The immediate application of this points to the Jews. They had rejected Jesus and would not sit at the Messiah's table; therefore, the lower classes of people, publicans, sinners, and even the heathen, would take their places at the royal table. Yet it is a wonderful truth of general application that God wants His house to be full, that He is abundant in mercy and desires the salvation of all. When once His invitation is refused, He returns again and goes to others in order that some will feast at His banquet. The Great Commission is world-wide. The Gospel is for all. The love of God desires a multitude of guests.

What a sight that was when the cripples and downcasts entered the banquet hall — the poor with their heads bowed, the lame leaning on their crutches, the blind groping around for a place to sit. But it was a happy group and a happy occasion. And what of those who did not come? They had closed themselves out. They had sent different excuses, yet there was only one reason why they did not come. They loved other things too much. They refused a generous host. They rejected grace.

THE PARABLE OF THE TOWER

"For which of you, desiring to build a tower, does not first sit down and count the cost, whether he has enough to complete it? Otherwise, when he has laid a foundation, and is not able to finish, all who see it begin to mock him, saying, 'This man began to build, and was not able to finish.'"

(Luke 14:28-30)

THE PARABLE OF THE KING

"Or what king, going to encounter another king in war, will not sit down first and take counsel whether he is able with ten thousand to meet him who comes against him with twenty thousand? And if not, while the other is yet a great way off, he sends an embassy and asks terms of peace. So therefore, whoever of you does not renounce all that he has cannot be my disciple."

(Luke 14:31-33)

16

COUNTING THE COST

The mark of a great leader is to state clearly the conditions that must be met by those who follow him. Jesus of Galilee was that kind of leader. Great multitudes had been following Him; many people were excited about Him. Some thought that as Messiah He would drive out the Roman horde. Others were fascinated by His strange teachings and His mighty works. Others were just curious. To this motley crowd that was turning the whole affair into a playful extravaganza, Jesus said: "If anyone comes to me and does not hate his father and mother, wife and children, brothers and sisters, even his own life, he cannot be my disciple. Whoever does not bear his own cross and come after Me, cannot be My disciple" (Luke 14:26-27). Crowding along behind Him did not mean discipleship, and Jesus with His stern language makes this unmistakably clear.

To further explain what He meant He chose two illustrations. The first illustration is that of a man who wanted to build a tower. The tower was most likely a vineyard tower (see Matthew 21:33). Quite often in a well-kept vineyard a tower was built to guard against those who might strip the vineyard in harvest time. Before a man began to build a tower, would he not sit down and figure out exactly what it was going to cost? Otherwise, when he began to build and could not finish, he would become a laughing-stock to all who saw him. Jesus as a carpenter had undoubtedly seen a number of men who began to build but ran out of funds before the job was completed. The other illustration is that of a king who contemplated war. Before engaging in a conflict, he calculates the odds and the risks involved. Is he able to stand against twenty thousand with his ten thousand? Are his own soldiers well-trained and eager for battle? Can he advantage himself somehow with the element of surprise? If he cannot afford to do battle, he must send a delegation and ask for peace.

The Hatred Jesus Demands

Before looking at these twin parables more closely, it is necessary to explore at greater length the kind of hatred Jesus demands. An easy and almost universal explanation is that Jesus did not intend for His words to be taken literally, that in reality He did not mean "hate" but rather "love less." But this interpretation, along with many similar interpretations of His strong statements, runs the risk of dulling the sharp edge of Jesus' command. What did Jesus mean when He said that we must hate our fathers and mothers and brothers and sisters? Concerning this paradox of hating others, several points should be noticed.

1. *The whole spirit of Jesus' teachings made it impossible that His disciples understand these words in their most literal meaning.* Jesus did not seek to crush the tender relationships of human friendships and love. Far from hating their friends, He called on His followers to love even their enemies (Matthew 5:43-48). He taught them that they must honor their parents and condemned the Pharisaic traditions that by-passed this solemn duty (Mark 7:9-13). He Himself when on the cross committed the care of His mother to a trusted friend (John 19:26-27). He spoke against anger and hatred of one's brother and said that it was a kind of murder (Matthew 5:21-26). Little children He gathered in His arms and blessed (Mark 10:13-16). His teachings and the warm context of His entire life made it quite clear that men were to be loved.

2. *The word "hate" is not to be taken to mean that we are to love our relatives and friends with a diminished love.* This would be opposed to the heart and soul of Christianity. Husbands are told to love their wives even as Christ loved the church (Ephesians 5:25). Christians are expected to cultivate "a sincere love of the brethren," and "to love one another earnestly from the heart" (1 Peter 1:22). It is true that we may love the Lord too little; but we cannot love any human being too much. And we shall never love the Lord more by loving our human friends less.

3. *The words "hate his own life also" supply the key to the problem.* A disciple is to hate his relatives and friends in the same sense that he hates himself. In what sense is a man to hate himself? He must hate whatever in himself is low and base, all that is greedy and selfish, anything that would drag him away from Christ and rob his real self of true values. In the same way he is to hate his relatives and friends. He ought to love them as he loves himself, and he ought to hate them as he hates himself. Whatever in them

is pure and right he is to love; whatever is unclean and self-indulgent he is to hate. And if a man's friends come to stand between him and his Lord, if a choice has to be made between natural affection and devotion to Christ, then true disciples must be ready to treat their dearest friends as hated enemies.

The Challenge of Christ

If Jesus' stern conditions of discipleship are regarded as determents to superficial enthusiasm, they may also be regarded as challenges to those whose ambition is to live an active and vigorous life. Jesus was uncompromisingly honest. He did not, like most recruiting-officers, keep back the difficult and dangerous in order to enlist men in His service. He wanted no one to come after Him under false illusions. Men would have to face up to the task or not follow Him at all.

So Jesus taught that men must count the cost if they wish to be His disciples. This is the lesson of the parables on the rash builder and the rash king. A man would be foolish to build a tower without estimating the cost; and a king would be foolish to go to war without taking into consideration the necessary risks. A man who desires to follow Christ must likewise see beforehand the hard and painful struggle that awaits him, and be ready to make the sacrifice required no matter what the cost. Before he begins the Christian life, a man should ask himself several questions.

1. *Am I willing to deny myself?* When a man starts out on the Christian way, it is the end of self. Self-denial is the first condition of discipleship. "If any man wants to come after me," Jesus said, "let him deny himself. . . ." (Matthew 16:24). By this Jesus did not mean a temporary denial of self, a sacrifice of certain pleasures for a week or two in order that some good cause might be supported. To deny oneself is to live no longer to please the self. The Apostle Paul wrote that he had been crucified with Christ (Galatians 2:20). He had killed self. He had nailed his passions and lusts to the cross. This is what he told the Colossian Christians that they must do (Colossians 3:5ff.). This is precisely what all men must do who sincerely seek Him. And it is a bitter treatment that is required. No death is easy. C. S. Lewis in his inimitable fashion has expressed it like this: "The Christian way is different. . . . Christ says, 'Give me all. I don't want so much of your time and so much of your money and so much of your work: I want you. I have not come to torment your natural self, but to kill it.

No half-measures are any good. I don't want to cut off a branch here and a branch there, I want to have the whole tree down. I don't want to drill the tooth, or crown it, or stop it, but to have it out. Hand over the whole natural self, all the desires which you think innocent as well as the ones you think wicked — the whole outfit. I will give you a new self instead. In fact, I will give you Myself: my own will shall become yours.' "[1] That is what Jesus requires. To deny self is in every moment and in every way to say no to self and yes to Jesus Christ.

2. *Am I willing to abide by His teachings?* Before starting out on the Christian way a man should ask if he is willing to live by Jesus' teachings. Along with this one needs to make sure that his mind is settled as to His claims. The Galilean, after all, made extraordinary claims. He was born to be a king (Matthew 2:2) and He told Pilate that He was a king (John 18:36). He professed to be the Christ, the Messiah foretold in the Old Testament (Mark 14:61-62; John 4:25-26). He said that He was the world's light (John 8:12); the one who could supply living water (John 4:10); the Bread of Life (John 6:35); the Way, the Truth and the Life (John 14:6). In short, He claimed to be the Savior of the world. These were preposterous claims even in that age. Any man would do well to review these claims once again and in this current age of doubt be convinced deep down in his heart that these claims are unequivocally true.

Commitment to Jesus' claims, however, involves living by His laws. True discipleship means continuing in the words of Christ (John 8:31). This is a vital part of the cost that must be counted. It is as though Jesus says to multitudes of His would-be followers: "You say you want to follow Me, but are you willing to do what I say? Are you willing to be guided solely by My teachings? Instead of an eye for an eye and a tooth for a tooth, are you prepared to turn the other cheek or go the second mile? Will you love those who hate you? When men persecute you, will you pray for them? Are you ready to exchange earthly treasures for heavenly treasures? Without reservations or any strings attached, are you really willing to put My kingdom first?" These are some of the awesome questions that Christ asks every man. They are questions that sift the multitudes. They are questions that try men's souls. The blueprint of the Christian life is laid out in microcosm in the Sermon on the Mount. Before a man calls himself a disciple, he must come to a definite and affirmative decision about that blueprint.

---

[1]C. S. Lewis, *Mere Christianity* (London: Fontana Books, 1955), pp. 163-64.

3. *Am I willing to follow Him to the end?* There are many people who are eager to follow Jesus as long as the way is easy and pleasant; but when the going gets hard and the road stretches long, they give it all up. The parable of the tower presents this as a distinct possibility for every Christian. Many Christians, like the reckless builder, start out with a spurt but never finish. They make their big mistake in thinking that the Christian race is only a short distance. But life's race is not a quick, snappy sprint. It is a marathon race, and there is danger present even on the last lap. Bunyan in his *Pilgrim's Progress* tells of one man who successfully completed the hazardous journey upward and then was turned away from the Celestial City.[2] This to Bunyan was a sign that there was a way to hell even from the gates of heaven. The Christian way lasts until the journey's end, and not until a man comes to know something of the toil and the length of that road has he fully counted the cost.

Facing the Facts

In every department of life it is good to be honest with oneself and face the facts. If a man wants to devote his life to others in the practice of medicine, there are many pleasures which are routine to others that he will have to forego. If he does not make allowances for this ahead of time, he will prove to be an eminently unhappy and unsuccessful doctor. If a man wishes to become a scholar, he must first realize that the road is tough, that it requires rigorous self-discipline and years of study alone in the night. A young man may have his heart set on becoming an athlete, he may envision numerous laurels of victory, but unless he is willing to pay the price for excellence no honors will ever be accorded him. Jesus in these parables does not intend to dampen enthusiasm, but He is saying that the hard facts of the Christian way must be faced or else red-hot enthusiasm will end up in cold despair. Nor does He mean in these parables that it is better not to begin than to begin and fail. He does mean, however, that it is better not to begin, than to begin with a flourish of trumpets and a look of glamour that invites disaster. There is no challenge that compares to the Christian life, and no thrill that exceeds the thrill of the Christian way, but dying with Him and taking up His cross is not easy. We must forsake all, and most of all we must forsake ourselves.

---

[2]John Bunyan, *The Pilgrim's Progress,* ed. Louis L. Martz (New York: Rinehart and Co., 1949), p. 168.

THE PARABLE OF THE LOST SHEEP

"Now the tax collectors and sinners were all drawing near to him. And the Pharisees and the scribes murmured, saying, 'This man receives sinners and eats with them.'

"So he told them this parable: 'What man of you, having a hundred sheep, if he has lost one of them, does not leave the ninety-nine in the wilderness, and go after the one which is lost, until he finds it? And when he has found it, he lays it on his shoulders, rejoicing. And when he comes home, he calls together his friends and his neighbors, saying to them, "Rejoice with me, for I have found my sheep which was lost." Even so, I tell you, there will be more joy in heaven over one sinner who repents than over ninety-nine righteous persons who need no repentance.'"

(Luke 15:1-7)
(Parallel Passage: Matthew 18:12-14)

THE PARABLE OF THE LOST COIN

"'Or what woman, having ten silver coins, if she loses one coin, does not light a lamp and sweep the house and seek diligently until she finds it? And when she has found it, she calls together her friends and neighbors, saying, "Rejoice with me, for I have found the coin which I had lost." Even so, I tell you, there is joy before the angels of God over one sinner who repents.'"

(Luke 15:8-10)

THE PARABLE OF THE PRODIGAL SON

"And he said, 'There was a man who had two sons; and the younger of them said to his father, "Father, give me the share of property that falls to me." And he divided his living between them. Not many days later, the younger son gathered all he had and took his journey into a far country, and there he squandered his property in loose living. And when he had spent everything, a great famine arose in that country, and he began to be in want. So he went and joined himself to one of the citizens of that country, who sent him into his fields to feed swine. And he would gladly have fed on the pods that the swine ate; and no one gave him anything. But when he came to himself he said, "How many of my father's hired servants have bread enough and to spare, but I perish here with hunger! I will arise and go to my father, and I will say to him, 'Father, I have sinned against heaven and before you; I am no longer worthy to be called your son; treat me as one of your hired servants.' " And he arose and came to his father. But while he was yet at a distance, his father saw him and had compassion, and ran and embraced him and kissed him. And the son said to him, "Father, I have sinned against heaven and before you; I am no longer worthy to be called your son." But the father said to his servants, "Bring quickly the best robe, and put it on him; and put a ring on his hand, and shoes on his feet; and bring the fatted calf and kill it, and let us eat and make merry; for this my son was dead, and is alive again; he was lost and is found." And they began to make merry.

" 'Now his elder son was in the field; and as he came and drew near to the house, he heard music and dancing. And he called one of the servants and asked what this meant. And he said to him, "Your brother has come, and your father has killed the fatted calf, because he has received him safe and sound." But he was angry and refused to go in. His father came out and entreated him, but he answered his father, "Lo, these many years I have served you, and I never disobeyed your command; yet you never gave me a kid, that I might make merry with my friends. But when this son of yours came, who has devoured your living with harlots, you killed for him the fatted calf." And he said to him, "Son, you are always with me, and all that is mine is yours. It was fitting to make merry and be glad, for this your brother was dead, and is alive; he was lost, and is found." ' "

(Luke 15:11-32)

17

"THIS MAN RECEIVES SINNERS"

The fifteenth chapter of Luke is perhaps the most priceless chapter in the Bible. Certainly no chapter is more tender and more lovely. For centuries it has been called "the Gospel in the Gospels," and the story of the prodigal boy who lost everything has been known as "the pearl of the parables."

This marvelous chapter has for its original audience the indignant scribes and Pharisees. They were not interested in the kingdom themselves, yet they were angered when they saw Jesus welcome the moral outcasts and black sheep of Jewish society. Their antagonism issued in bitter criticism and they sneered: "This fellow receives sinners and eats with them." And what does Jesus say in His defense? He does not respond with a hot protest. Rather He concedes the absolute truth of the charge, and on the basis of it presents a touching lesson in parables. The parables are three in number, with one parable including in its story another parable. Although three parables, they present one picture and they read as one continued essay on the subject of God's compassion for the lost.

The Sheep and the Coin

The first picture that Jesus sketches is that of a shepherd and his sheep. The Palestinian sheep was then and is today the so-called "broad-tailed sheep." The tails of these sheep are extremely large and weigh on an average from ten to fifteen pounds each. These sheep have always been valuable to their owners. To many of the Jews in ancient times, sheep represented their chief wealth and their sole means of livelihood. Sheep provided food to eat (1 Samuel 14:23), milk to drink (Isaiah 7:21-22), wool for the making of cloth (Job 31:20), and flesh for the offering of numerous sacrifices (Exodus 12:5-6; 20:24; Leviticus 1:10). Because the sheep were by nature wayward and defenseless, it was necessary that they have constant supervision. In both Old and New Testaments the close relationship of God and His people is projected in the winsome figure of the shepherd and his sheep (Psalms 100:3; 23:1; Isaiah 40:11; Matthew 9:36). Thus as we read of the selfless shepherd who went out searching through the hills for one stray lamb, we should remember that Jesus Christ Himself is the supremely Good Shepherd who was willing to die for His sheep (John 10:1-18).

The second picture is that of a woman who lost a coin. The coin specified by Luke was a Greek *drachma,* which was almost equivalent to a Roman *denarius.* It was a silver coin, and although worth by our standards less than twenty cents, it was the common wage for a day's labor. Some scholars have suggested that in this case the coin was especially valuable to the woman since it formed an ornament for her head. It was customary for Jewish women to save up ten coins and string them together for a necklace or hairdress. The ornament became a treasured possession worn as the sign of a married woman, very much like a wedding band is worn today. At any rate, whether as a part of her cherished jewelry or simply as something of monetary worth, the coin was of priceless value to the woman. That is evident from her diligent search. On missing the coin, she at once lit her little oil lamp and began to sweep. A lamp was necessary for the search even in daytime, for houses then were usually built without windows and with only one door. In the house there was no wood or stone flooring, only the packed earth covered with dried reeds and rushes. With a floor like this, there were many places where a coin could be lodged. All of this made the search a difficult and trying experience and helps explain why the woman was overjoyed when she found the silver piece that had been lost.

The Lost Son

The third picture that Jesus gives is that of a son. Under Jewish law the terms by which a man assigned his inheritance were quite specific. The law clearly stated that the first-born son was to receive a "double portion" of the father's property (Deuteronomy 21:17). This would mean in this case that two-thirds of the property belonged to the older son and one-third to the younger son. Often a father disposed of his possessions before he died. At the same time he conferred blessings on his sons, and these blessings were regarded as irrevocable. In the parable the younger son went to his father and demanded the part of the inheritance that was his. He wanted it right then. He could not wait. Later, after running through his fortune in the far country, he was forced to go into the field and feed swine. Since the swine were unclean animals (Leviticus 11:7), to a Jew this was the most degrading and humiliating task possible. The husks that the young man desired to eat were the pods of the carob tree, a tree that is still common in Palestine and neighboring countries. When the young man decided to return home, he intended to ask his father to treat him as a hired servant. The word used here is *misthios*, which means a *hired man*, a *day laborer*. A hired man worked only a day at a time. He had no guarantee of employment and lived on the thin edge of starvation. So a deliberate contrast in this parable is that the young man left home as a prince and returned home to be a lowly day laborer.

Lost Men

It is good for us to try to explore these parables more fully. What do they mean? What lessons did Jesus intend to teach? In these parables Jesus taught *that men are lost*. It is interesting to note that Jesus seldom called men "sinners." Rather He spoke of them as being "lost" (Matthew 10:6; 15:24; 18:11). It was not that He counted them as moral wretches or outlaws in headstrong rebellion against their Maker. It was simply that men were misguided and disillusioned and needed to be set back on the right course.

There are different ways by which men become lost.

1. *Sometimes a man gets lost like a sheep is lost.* A sheep is a senseless and careless animal. It wanders here and there. It is apt to go any place where there is an opening. It strays off into the distant hills and does not know the way back home. It does not know that it is lost. Multitudes of people are like this. They do not revolt against God, they do not fight against His church. They edge away from Him step by step. They put aside their Bibles, close their prayer-closets, and stop attending the church services. They slip away with the tide of the world and become spiritually numb. Thus the writer of the Hebrew letter warns: "We must pay the closer attention to what we have heard, lest we drift away from it" (Hebrews 2:1). Like the heedless sheep, many men drift away from Christ.

2. *Sometimes a man is lost like the coin was lost.* The coin did not get lost through its own fault, but because of the fault of someone else. The woman carelessly let the coin slip through her fingers. There is a difference, of course, between coins and people. The

coin was in no sense responsible for being lost. But with men there is always the responsibility of choice that governs destiny. So the coin was lost in a sense that man can never be. However, it is true that many lives end in shipwreck not primarily because of their own mistakes but because of the mistakes of others.

3. *Sometimes a man is lost like the younger son was lost.* The son was lost not through his own carelessness or through the carelessness of others. He took his journey to the far country with set purpose and aforethought. He turned away from home thinking of no one but himself. He never once considered the feelings of his father. Although he did not leave to hurt his father intentionally, still he was willing to break his heart in order to get his own way. Self-will is the root of sin, and it is the downfall of many souls. Deliberately, with their eyes open, many people forsake the church and go off into the land of God-forgetfulness. They throw away all restraint and violate whatever law they choose; they will eat and drink and be merry, regardless. This is the essence of sin. To desire to please self in spite of the consequences, to do what one wants to do regardless of the feelings of others, to pursue the will of self instead of the will of God, this is the heart of sin and the sin of sins. Of all the characters of literature, the younger son stands at the head of the list of those who make self-pleasing their rule of life.

God's Attitude toward the Lost

But the main emphasis of these parables is not simply that men are lost. An even more important lesson is brought to light: *God's attitude toward lost men.* God's attitude toward those in sin is the same attitude that Jesus had. Jesus received sinners, and this was the very thing that the Jews could not understand. They believed that God was merciful to the righteous, but they were quite sure that He had nothing to do with sinners. The great lesson of these parables, however, is that God desires more than anything else that sinners come to Him. This is shown by:

1. *The search.* God's attitude toward the lost is seen in the diligent search of the shepherd and of the woman. It is one thing to accept sinners, it is another thing to go out and look for them. A woman drops a coin. She lights a lamp and sweeps the house; she will not rest until she finds it. God is like that in His search for men. A shepherd loses one sheep from his flock. What is to be done? He leaves the ninety-nine sheep that are safe and goes out

looking for it. God is like that shepherd. He wants men; and when one is lost, He goes out and finds it. He does not drive it back or hire someone to carry it back, but like the shepherd puts it on His own shoulders and brings it home. However mean and base men may be, God still wants them.

2. *The joy.* God's attitude toward the lost is seen in His joy. It is a basic point in these parables that the shepherd, the woman, and the father were filled with uncontrollable joy when they gained again what had been lost. The Pharisees had a saying, "There is joy before God when those who provoke Him perish from the world."[1] But Jesus said that there is joy in heaven before the angels of God when one sinner repents. God is kind. He is more understanding than men. He does not dismiss the tax-collectors as worthless. He feels deep in His heart the joy of joys when one wanderer returns home.

Lost but Saved

In the parable of the prodigal, Jesus tells us about a young man who threw away his life and yet was reclaimed. The downward path of the boy begins when he goes to his father to get his inheritance. He feels that he has been baby of the family long enough, and that it is time for him to strike out on his own. The father does not try to dissuade him. Anxieties that were couched in his heart, he left unexpressed. He simply let him go. And the young man left with scarcely any delay. He was off to see the world, he would be his own master, he would please himself even if it was an affront to a gracious father.

1. *What he lost.* But the consequences of self-pleasing are always bitter. The son found out by disastrous experience what countless millions have had to learn: sin carries in itself its own penalties.

What did this young man lose when he journeyed into a far country? First, he lost the *fellowship of his father* and *the comforts of home.* He had lived in the best house, with the best servants to wait on him, under the guidance of the best father a boy could have. But all of these things meant nothing to him until he was left friendless in a strange land. A thousand miles away he dreamed of home, of his comrades in youth, and of his good father.

[1]Alfred Plummer, *A Critical and Exegetical Commentary on the Gospel According to St. Luke* (*International Critical Commentary* series; New York: Charles Scribner's Sons, n.d.) p. 371.

In a far country these things were dear to him, but out of his reach.

Second, he lost his *self-respect*. What a paradox that the young man who left home full of confidence and self-esteem was forced to go to the fields and feed swine. The boy who flung away his family because of pride ends up sleeping with swine. How different he looks now in the swine-field from that bright, clear morning when he rode away from home like a prince at the head of a caravan! His pride is shattered in the dust of the swine paths. He is unknown and unheeded and unwanted in the far country.

Third, he lost *all that he had*. The story says that he spent everything. The inheritance that he had received so easily he squandered easily. When he had run through his fortune and gone bankrupt, calamity struck. "A great famine arose in that country, and he began to be in want." There is, of course, always a famine in the land where God is forgotten. He finds himself alone, for his friends have deserted him. He sees now that they were not real friends. Nor were his pleasures true pleasures. They did not last.

> Pleasures are like poppies spread;
> You seize the flower, its bloom is shed.
> Or like the snow falls in the river,
> A moment white — then melts forever.[2]

What will the prodigal do? Will he go home? No, not he; he will bear it out to the end. He takes employment from a foreign citizen. The citizen *sends* him to the field; now he has lost even his freedom. In fact, he has lost his independence, his pride, his fortune — everything he counted dear and for which he left home to obtain. Alone with the swine he sobs out his confession, "I perish with hunger!"

2. *How he was saved*. But this young man comes back. What were the steps on his upward journey that led him to his father? First, *self-evaluation*. "He came to himself." He said, "What a fool I've been. Back at home there is plenty of food. Even the servants have more to eat than I do." He was out of his mind when he left his father. He sees himself now for the first time. It is a great hour when a man comes to himself, when a man is willing to face the honest facts about himself. This is the beginning point of a man's return to God.

---

[2]Robert Burns, *Tam o' Shanter*.

Second, *decision.* Having faced himself, the young man came to a decision. He said, "I will arise and go to my father." It was a great moment. It was a decision that for days he had pushed out of his mind. But now that he saw himself clearly, he saw his father in a differe. t light. When we see ourselves as we are, our personal inventory sh. ild lead us to a decision of character.

Third, *action.* "He said, I will arise. . . . *And he arose.*" He did not delay. He id not hesitate between saying and doing. He would not be tu. ned aside or tempted to reconsider. He made up his mind to go, and he went. Many today are not in the body of Christ because they have floundered between the saying and the doing.

Fourth, *confession.* When the young man reached a decision, he worked out his confession. There would be no mincing of words or jabbering of excuses. He would speak the full truth. "Father, I have sinned against heaven and before you; I am no longer worthy to be called your son; treat me as one of your hired servants." Overwhelmed by his unworthiness, he only wants to be treated like a lowly day-laborer. He regards his sins, grievous as they were, as committed mainly against heaven and against his father. We, too, when we sin, should say like David, "Against thee, thee only, have I sinned" (Psalms 51:4).

But the confession of the humble, penitent son was cut short in the embrace of a loving father. What a painful journey it was to return home gaunt, barefooted, in rags and shame. As the prodigal rounds the bend in the road, his father recognizes him. He had been looking for him through all the sad years. He runs to him. Why did he not preserve his dignity and wait for his son to come to him? He could not! He ran to him and fell on his neck and kissed him. "Wait a minute, father," the son says. "I have sinned against heaven, I have sinned against you. . . ." But love is so eager to receive that it does not seek explanations. The father beckons to the servants: "Bring quickly the best robe, and put it on him; and put a ring on his hand, and shoes on his feet; and bring the fatted calf and kill it, and let us eat and make merry; for this my son was dead, and is alive again; he was lost, and is found."

Saved but Lost

There is another picture in the story. The other son is out in the field. What kind of person was he? It may be that at times we deal too harshly with him.

1. *He was self-righteous.* He could find nothing good in the life of his brother. Everything his brother had done was bad. As for himself, he was proud of his work and proud of his life. He had worked all these years and he had not transgressed a single commandment. He was very much like the Pharisees who criticized Jesus because He received sinners.

2. *He was jealous.* He would not go in and greet his brother, but sulked outside the house. His father went out to him and entreated him. And what does he say? "You never gave *me* a kid, but look what you gave *him*." Of course, he had missed the mark a mile. Not just a kid, but all that the father had was his.

3. *He was heartless.* He was not at all happy that his brother had come home. He had rather have his brother beaten than be forgiven. His whole outlook is one of disdain and contempt. He could not see that if his father had gained a son, he had gained a brother.

We do not deal more harshly with the older brother than the story itself. Surely no character of the Bible is more unlovely than he. The lesson of the parable is severe. It is not necessary for one to go on a long journey in order to leave God. One can stay at home — not know his Father and not know his Father's heart — and be lost at home as well as anywhere else. As Augustine prayed long ago: "It is not by our feet, or change of place, that men leave Thee. . . . in lustful — that is, in darkened — affections, is the true distance from Thy face."[3]

God Misses Each One

The three parables unite in teaching that God misses even one that is lost. This is true because God is a Father, and a father cannot rest until all his children are safe and secure. A father of twenty children is sad if one is missing. So God as a Father cannot spare even one. He misses each one. He yearns for his return.

> Helpless and foul as the trampled snow,
> Sinner, despair not! Christ stoopeth low
> To rescue the soul that is lost in sin,
> And raise it to life and enjoyment again.[4]

There is much hope, if one's repentance, like the prodigal's, is as genuine as his fall. What a delightful sight when a prodigal returns to his Father's heart and home!

[3]Augustine, *Confessions* I. 28.
[4]"Beautiful Snow," Author Unknown.

THE PARABLE OF THE DISHONEST STEWARD

"He also said to the disciples, 'There was a rich man who had a steward, and charges were brought to him that this man was wasting his goods. And he called him and said to him, "What is this that I hear about you? Turn in the account of your stewardship, for you can no longer be steward." And the steward said to himself, "What shall I do, since my master is taking the stewardship away from me? I am not strong enough to dig, and I am ashamed to beg. I have decided what to do, so that people may receive me into their houses when I am put out of the stewardship." So, summoning his master's debtors one by one, he said to the first, "How much do you owe my master?" He said, "A hundred measures of oil." And he said to him, "Take your bill, and sit down quickly and write fifty." Then he said to another, "And how much do you owe?" He said, "A hundred measures of wheat." He said to him, "Take your bill, and write eighty." The master commended the dishonest steward for his prudence; for the sons of this world are wiser in their own generation than the sons of light. And I tell you, make friends for yourselves by means of unrighteous mammon, so that when it fails they may receive you into the eternal habitations.

"'He who is faithful in a very little is faithful also in much; and he who is dishonest in a very little is dishonest also in much. If then you have not been faithful in the unrighteous mammon, who will entrust to you the true riches? And if you have not been faithful in that which is another's, who will give you that which is your own? No servant can serve two masters; for either he will hate the one and love the other, or he will be devoted to the one and despise the other. You cannot serve God and mammon.'"

(Luke 16:1-13)

18

CHRISTIAN PRUDENCE

"The master commended the dishonest steward for his prudence." These are strange and difficult words, for they are spoken of a man who was a fraud, a trickster and a thief. Why was he commended? What lessons are to be gained by studying his schemes and watching his quick moves? Surely we need to examine this parable of Jesus very carefully.

The main character in the story is a steward who had been put in charge of a rich man's estate. The steward was probably a slave who by past service had proved himself trustworthy. As manager of the affairs, he had complete and absolute authority over everything. In time rumors reached the master's ears, and he found that his trusted slave all along had been stealing from him. At once he summoned the steward. It was a critical time. What was the steward to do? He could not establish his innocence. He had grown very careless, never anticipating that such a day would come. Was he to do manual labor? No; his hands were too soft for that. Could he find other work? There was little chance of that, for who would hire someone who had stolen from his master? Was he to beg? No; he had too much pride. He was ashamed to beg, but he was not ashamed to steal. In a flash he saw that the only way out was to steal again! He called in his master's debtors. One man owed a hundred measures of oil.[1] The steward told him to take the bill and write that he owed only fifty measures. Another man owed a hundred measures of wheat; he was told to change it to eighty.[2] In this way the steward altered the accounts of all of his master's debtors. His plan was a simple one: by falsifying the records he figured to gain the gratitude of the debtors, so that when he was let out of his job he would be repaid by the hospitality of his friends. When his master learned of the plot, instead of burning with anger, he shrugged his shoulders and with a cynical grin

---

[1]The measure mentioned was a *bath,* an amount equal to about five and a half American gallons.

[2]The measure here was a *cor,* equal to about five bushels.

commended the steward for his sharp practice. So all the characters in the story were rogues and rascals. The steward was dishonest; he had been systematically stealing from his master, and even after being caught continued to lie and steal his way out. The debtors were, of course, dishonest; they immediately seized the opportunity to take advantage of their creditor and registered their names on fictitious entries. The master also was a worldly rascal, a man who was able to appreciate a shifty bit of work even when directed against himself.

Some Points of Interpretation

The parable presents indeed a peculiar story, one that has been long regarded as difficult to explain. From the outset a few points should be made clear, which aid in the interpretation of the parable.

1. *The parable, although told in story form, is simply illustrative.* It is not different in kind from the story of the Good Samaritan or the parable about the Prodigal Son. In each of these many details are given, but the details are added only to give force to the illustration. We are not to ask who the robbers or the innkeeper or the Samaritan represent. Likewise, in this parable we should not attach special meaning to each person and each detail. Failing to recognize this, interpreters of the past have tried, for example, to make the steward stand for such as Pilate, Judas, Satan, the Apostle Paul, and Christ Himself. But the steward, the rich man, and the debtors stand for no one in particular. The parable seeks to convey one central truth, and all details of the parable must be understood in light of that truth.

2. *The phrase "mammon of unrighteousness" has been made unnecessarily difficult.* The word "mammon" is an Aramaic word which means "money" or "wealth." "Mammon of unrighteousness" is a descriptive phrase that means, as the Revised Standard Version has put it, "unrighteous mammon." "Unrighteous mammon" has been taken by some to mean wealth gained by dishonest means such as by violence or fraud. But surely Jesus does not mean that we are to make friends by means of unjust gain. Others have said that "unrighteous mammon" refers not so much to money gained illegally but to money that somehow in itself is tainted with evil, that there is a certain defilement necessarily attached to money. But the probable explanation of the problem is found in verse 12, where "unrighteous mammon" is contrasted with the "true riches."

True riches are those values that are permanent and enduring; thus unrighteous mammon simply would be the untrue, the uncertain riches, the riches that cannot be trusted.

3. *The commendation of the dishonest steward, it should be emphasized, came from his master.* Many people get the wrong idea when they read: "And the lord commended the unjust steward, because he had done wisely" (verse 8, King James Version). Here "the lord" does not mean "the Lord Jesus Christ," but it refers to the lord of the steward, the steward's master. Had the steward acted wisely? Not really, and so the Revised Standard Version reads: "The master commended the dishonest steward for his prudence."

Christian Prudence

Cunning and deceitful though he was, the steward is held up by Jesus as an example of Christian prudence. He said, "The sons of this world are wiser [more prudent] in their own generation than the sons of light." By this He meant that children of the world, those whose hopes are centered in material goods, have more energy and foresight in the exercise of their material concerns than Christians have in the practice of Christianity. The point is, as summarized in the words of Trench, that Christians "bestow less pains to win heaven than *'the children of this world'* bestow to win earth, — that they are less provident in heavenly things than those are in earthly, — that the world is better served by its servants than God is by his."[3] Certainly that is the chief lesson of the parable. The steward bent every effort to provide for his future welfare; the debtors hastened to join in with the scheme of a crafty thief; and the master was ready to wink at their dishonesty. If only Christians were as diligent and resourceful in kingdom business as business men are in worldly business!

This chief lesson of the parable can be illustrated in various ways. Here is a man who is a golfer. He travels the circuit week after week to make a mark for himself. Before each tournament he surveys the course with scrupulous care. He practices and perfects every shot. He knows how to "fade" and "hook"; he knows when to play it safe and when to go for the pin. No matter how skilled he may be, he never plays a round without practice; and often after eighteen holes he returns to the practice tee for more work on his game. Or take as another example the life insurance salesman.

---

[3]Trench, *Notes on the Parables of Our Lord,* p. 443.

He studies the basic principles of salesmanship. He goes about looking for prospects; and when he finds a likely candidate, he stays with him. He calls on him time and again. He has learned that persistence pays off. If only Christians were as devoted to heavenly things as the golfer is to sharpening his strokes; if only Christians were as persistent in the pursuit of souls as the salesman is in the pursuit of money — the contrast is striking and shameful. So in this parable Jesus is saying, "Look at the way worldly men pursue their ambitions. If they are so eager about uncertain riches, why aren't *you* more enthusiastic about the true values?" The children of the world are more prudent than the children of light.

The Management of Money

While the basic aim of the parable is to teach on Christian prudence, Jesus also uses it to teach other truths. He says, "Make friends for yourselves by means of unrighteous mammon, so that when it fails they may receive you into the eternal habitations." The expression "they may receive you" should not be pressed too far. It is merely another way of saying that if men use money in the right way, they will be received at last in heaven.

Jesus had much to say about money. In His characteristically practical way He had to give attention to man's enduring problem of the handling of money. Jesus knew that almost everything in life is measured by money. He felt it necessary, therefore, that men have a right attitude toward it. In this parable, then, what does Jesus teach concerning material wealth? First, He says that material wealth is temporary. Unrighteous mammon is contrasted with the true riches: the true riches endure, material things do not last. Second, Jesus reminds us that our material wealth is not our own. "If you have not been faithful in that which is another's. . . ." Even while we have it, it belongs to someone else. We have no real title to it. Its tenure is precarious; we cannot count on it for a single day. We did not bring it into the world, nor will we take it with us when we leave. It is not a part of us; we are not a part of it. It may go any day; it *will* go one day.

Third, Jesus teaches us that material wealth must be used wisely. Money is not a part of man. It is an adjunct, a *tool* that must be used in the right way. There are two very basic attitudes toward money. One attitude is that *man can allow money to be his master*. Man can become the slave of money. This is what happens in the case of the miser. The miser hoards all that he can get his hands on.

Very recently it happened that a man called on another in the interest of raising money for a school. The man, well advanced in years, was quite wealthy, and was a citizen of the town where the school was located. One day after repeated visits had been made, the result being that not one penny had been promised to the school, the man confided in his friend. He knew, he said, that one day soon he was going to have to part with his money; but his money gave him so much pleasure that he could not bear the thought of it. Each evening after he closed his store, he related, he went up to his hotel room, took out his money, and ran it through his fingers. That was the only happiness that he knew. But the miser is not the only one who becomes enslaved to money. Let us remember that this happens to the man, *any man,* who sets the making of money above all things in life. It is well to keep in mind, as someone has pointed out, that "money can cost too much."

The other attitude toward money is that *man can use it in the service of God.* The grand truth underlying the whole parable is that Christians are stewards of another's possessions. That is to say, we are managers of the things that belong to God. In a very literal sense everything that we have and are — our education, our thoughts and deeds, our wealth, everything — is God's. Then it is most reasonable to use whatever is in our hands in His service. In fact, we will be found to be dishonest stewards if we selfishly treasure what is not ours. If we use our money wisely, it is to say that the supreme values in life are always human and spiritual. We never use our money in the right way until we use it in the service of God.

Fidelity in Service

Jesus attaches other lessons to this parable. He says, "He who is faithful in a very little is faithful also in much." If Christians are stewards, then it is expected of them that they be faithful (see 1 Corinthians 4:2). What does this fidelity demand? It requires that Christians be faithful in small things as well as large. If they cannot prove themselves, Jesus says, in the small things, who will commit to them the true riches? True fidelity means that Christians must continue in choosing God instead of mammon. In Biblical times no slave could serve two masters. A slave was owned absolutely by his lord; every minute of his time and every ounce of his energy belonged to him. So the Christian cannot serve God in a part-time capacity. God and mammon are uncompromising opposites. Mam-

mon may demand, for instance, a treasuring up, while God may
desire a scattering abroad. Mammon says a man is a success according to what he *gets*; God says a man is blessed if he *gives*. One
must be despised if the other is to be loved. To be faithful to one
means utter separation from the other. Faithful stewards are the
kind of stewards that both God and men need.

A Final Audit

Thus from a set of worldly rascals Jesus teaches great lessons.
The men in the parable believed in things; they sought for and
were absorbed in things. Nothing else mattered. The Christian, to
the contrary, believes in the spiritual. He seeks the Kingdom first.
Yet in all of his seeking he will miss the Kingdom, according to
Jesus, if he does not pursue it with the industry and forethought of
the dishonest steward. As the steward was summoned in, so the
Christian will be summoned to render account of his stewardship.
One last audit awaits every Christian.

THE PARABLE OF THE RICH MAN AND LAZARUS

" 'There was a rich man, who was clothed in purple and fine linen and who feasted sumptuously every day. And at his gate lay a poor man named Lazarus, full of sores, who desired to be fed with what fell from the rich man's table; moreover the dogs came and licked his sores. The poor man died and was carried by the angels to Abraham's bosom. The rich man also died and was buried; and in Hades, being in torment, he lifted up his eyes, and saw Abraham far off and Lazarus in his bosom. And he called out, "Father Abraham, have mercy upon me, and send Lazarus to dip the end of his finger in water and cool my tongue; for I am in anguish in this flame." But Abraham said, "Son, remember that you in your lifetime received your good things, and Lazarus in like manner evil things, but now he is comforted here, and you are in anguish. And besides all this, between us and you a great chasm has been fixed, in order that those who would pass from here to you may not be able, and none may cross from there to us." And he said, "Then I beg you, father, to send him to my father's house, for I have five brothers, so that he may warn them, lest they also come into this place of torment." But Abraham said, "They have Moses and the prophets; let them hear them." And he said, "No, father Abraham; but if some one goes to them from the dead, they will repent." He said to them, "If they do not hear Moses and the prophets, neither will they be convinced if some one should rise from the dead." ' "

(Luke 16:19-31)

19

A GLIMPSE INTO ETERNITY

Albert Schweitzer in one of his books relates that this story started a revolution in his heart. He came to regard Africa as a beggar lying at Europe's doorstep, and so he felt that it was his mission to go to the Dark Continent. The story in Luke 16 is indeed a story that moves men to action. One can hardly read it without wondering if perhaps there might be at his own gates a neglected soul that he has never seen.

The question has often been raised whether this is a parable or an actual historical account. Some believe that it should not be understood as a parable. They point out that there is nothing in Luke's record to indicate that it is a parable, that, to the contrary, Jesus said, "There was a certain rich man." But the same can be said of the previous parable on the dishonest steward. Jesus began that story with exactly the same words, "There was a certain rich man" (Luke 16:1). It is not likely that the words should be taken figuratively in one part of the chapter and literally in another. In addition, the story of the rich man and Lazarus stands in a series of parables that reaches from Luke 14 through chapter 18. The two parables in chapter 16 are perfectly complementary to each other. They both concern the right use of money: the one showing how a wise use of wealth can secure a happy reception in heaven, the other showing how a selfish use of wealth can lead to anguish and misery in eternity.

The parable at hand is unique in at least one respect: it gives a name to one of its characters. The rich man is often known as *Dives,* which is the Latin word for rich; but this name is not a part of the parable. Jesus, however, does describe a neglected beggar and names him *Lazarus.* Lazarus was a common name, being the Greek form for the Hebrew name Eleazar. Eleazar means "God is my help," and no doubt Jesus selected this name to show that God is the helper of those who call on Him.

Three Scenes

Jesus relates the story of the rich man and Lazarus in three scenes. There is, first, a brief picture of the two men as they lived on earth. The rich man lived in ease and luxury. He was clothed in purple and fine linen. In the ancient world purple garments were the garments of royalty and were considered a sign of honor and wealth (see Judges 8:26; Esther 8:15; Daniel 5:7). Each day the man feasted magnificently. This is what the King James Version means when it says that he "fared sumptuously." Every day he ate in royal style and arrayed himself in royal robes.

It was a very beautiful scene except for one eyesore. At the edge of the picture, outside the gates of the palace, was a lowly beggar. He was hungry, he would gladly eat anything that came from the rich man's table. He was sick. His body was covered with loathsome ulcers. He was so weak and helpless that he could not defend himself against the dogs that licked his sores. The contrast of these two men on earth, the rich man and the beggar, is sharp and painfully tragic.

The second scene is of the two men in death. Weak and sick and hungry, it was not long till the beggar died. Was he missed? Were there friends to comfort him in the last hours? Was he extended the courtesy of a burial?

> Rattle his bones over the stones,
> He's but a pauper whom nobody owns.

The rich man also died. Everybody expected the beggar to die, but not the rich man, not the leading citizen in the town. But, like the beggar, he died. All the money that he had could not bribe away death. He died in spite of his wealth; he died in spite of his palace and fine clothes. And he was buried. What a funeral it must have been, with the gathering of crowds, the lament of mourners, and the reading of eulogies. Thus the curtain falls on the second scene of the story.

The third scene reveals the fate of the two men after death. Lazarus died and was "carried by the angels to Abraham's bosom." The expression is figurative and suggests the deep fellowship of Abraham with all his true descendants: he receives them like a father encloses a child in his arms. Lazarus, therefore, was in a state of complete bliss.

The rich man, wondering where he was, lifted up his eyes in Hades. Now stripped of his purple robe, in torment, he was experiencing a foretaste of hell. When convinced that this was really himself and not a dream, he began to plead for mercy. The rich man had become a beggar. He had sought to save his life and had lost it.

What Death Does Not Do

The parable as told by Jesus conveys great lessons concerning the life that now is and the life that is to come. It would be utterly wrong to attempt to construct, on the basis of this one parable, a detailed, inflexible theology of the after-life. The great temptation to dogmatize concerning the unknown should be avoided. Nevertheless Jesus has given us a brief look into the other world, from which there emerge certain unmistakable lessons. We learn from Him that there are certain things that death, with all of its power, *cannot* do.

1. *Death cannot destroy consciousness.* The rich man and Lazarus are dead, and yet they are vividly alive. They are not asleep or unaware of what is about them. They are conscious.

The fact of consciousness after death is made very clear in the parable, but it is also clear from other portions of Scripture. On one occasion Jesus silenced the Sadducees, who did not believe in the resurrection, by referring to the Old Testament (see Matthew 22:23-33). He reminded them that God said to Moses, "I am the God of Abraham, and the God of Isaac, and the God of Jacob." This was long after the great patriarchs had died. Yet, Jesus adds, "God is not the God of the dead, but of the living." It is absurd to think that God rules over those who have no existence; therefore, Abraham, Isaac, and Jacob must still be living. In other places Jesus taught that consciousness survives death. He said, for example, of the wicked who rejected Him and disregarded His will: "They will go away into eternal punishment" (Matthew 25:46). The place of condemnation is a place of pain and suffering. But where there is no consciousness there is no suffering; so men are conscious after death.

2. *Death cannot destroy identity.* The rich man and Lazarus were not only alive, but they were conscious of being themselves. The rich man was still the rich man and Lazarus was still Lazarus. The rich man speaks of himself as being the same person; he knows that he is the same individual that knew Lazarus in life; and he knows that he is of a family of six brothers.

Now it is true that death changes many things. At death we are severed from all things material. Our monetary gains, our treasures, all of our possessions are wrenched from our hands. Our earthly houses are dissolved. Our bodies return to indistinguishable forms of dust. Everything that is physical perishes. But death cannot change personality. The individual self lives on.

It is remarkable how many people think that death will work for them a marvelous transformation. They feel that they can stain their lives in the slush pits of sin, and by the mere act of dying go into the presence of God as white as snow. But it is not possible to lie down one moment selfish, sinful, godless, and in the next moment after death be altogether pure and sinless and Christlike. Death's last breath cannot alter a bad character or a guilty conscience. Only the blood of Christ can cleanse a man's heart and purge his life. Death will not do for a sin-swamped soul what His blood could not do. As death finds a man, so he will be the instant after when he opens his eyes in the unseen world. You will be yourself, and I will be myself. We are ourselves and will be ourselves eternally.

3. *Death cannot destroy memory.* In Hades the rich man sought relief from his anguish. But Abraham said, "Son, remember. . . ." Abraham wanted him to look back and see the kind of person he was on earth. He *could* remember. He remembered his life of self-pleasing. He remembered Lazarus. He remembered his five brothers. After death, then, men will have the power of memory. The power of memory will deepen and magnify the joys of heaven; and it will also agonize the conscience and intensify the regrets of those condemned in a devil's hell.

4. *Death cannot destroy destiny.* In this story Jesus plainly teaches us that after death there are only two rewards. Lazarus found himself in a place of joy and comfort. The rich man, however, was in bitter pain. He cries that Lazarus might be sent to touch his finger in water and cool his tongue. Even the smallest assistance would be welcomed. In the unseen realm there is a sharp separation between the godlike and the godless. There is a great gulf fixed. The Greek word for gulf is *chasma,* which is the same word as the English word *chasm.* Thus between the righteous and the wicked there is a huge chasm or abyss. And that chasm is fixed. The Greek word for *fixed,* if rendered literally, would be translated "has been and remains fixed." The division of the good and the bad is absolutely fixed and permanent.

Who separated the rich man and Lazarus? Who fixed the chasm that divided them? Not God, not Christ, not the angels. These men separated themselves. While on earth there was a great chasm that marked them off from each other. They made different choices. They traveled different roads. They lived in different worlds. And that chasm that existed on earth, unchanged by death, continued on into eternity.

The Rich Man's Condemnation

In the parable the rich man was irrevocably consigned to the place of torment. What wrongs were in his life? Why was he condemned? He was not condemned simply because he was rich or because he lived in a fine house. Not all rich people are censured by the Lord, for Abraham himself was rich. Nor was the rich man condemned because of any outright wickedness. He was not a violent man. He was not deliberately cruel to Lazarus. He did not drive him away from his gates, or slap him in the face as he passed him by. What, then, were the sins of the rich man?

1. *He was indifferent.* How long did Lazarus remain at the rich man's gate? We do not know, but long enough for the rich man in the afterlife to recognize Lazarus in Abraham's bosom. Time and time again the rich man had seen Lazarus begging outside his house. There right in front of him was a man sick and starving to death. That man was his responsibility. He could have emptied his pockets one day and laid up treasures in heaven. His wealth could have been the means of securing his salvation. But he was calloused to human distress, even with a man at his front door.

2. *He was selfish.* The problem of the rich man went deeper than indifference. Lying behind his cold unconcern was a self-centered life occupied with pleasures. His physical enjoyments were his chief pride. Absorbed in them, he became mercilessly oblivious to the needs of others. Selfishness degraded his life and sealed his doom.

3. *He minimized the written word.* When the rich man found out that no relief was possible for him, he asked that someone be sent to warn his five brothers. Abraham replied: "They have Moses and the prophets; let them hear them." "No, father Abraham," he said, "that is not enough." It is as though to say, "If I had been rightly warned, if something else had been offered to me besides Moses and the prophets, I would have listened." Thus on earth the rich man made light of the word of God. He had looked on it as powerless and peripheral. But Abraham said that God's written message was as effective as a voice from the dead.

Men are not saved by the witness of ghosts. They are not convinced through miracles but by persuasion. God draws men to Christ through the teaching of His word (John 6:44-45). The word of God when believed and received is able to save from sin (James 1:21). To underestimate its value is to put oneself in jeopardy of everlasting rejection.

THE PARABLE OF THE PHARISEE AND THE PUBLICAN

"He also told this parable to some who trusted in themselves that they were righteous and despised others: 'Two men went up into the temple to pray, one a Pharisee and the other a tax collector. The Pharisee stood and prayed thus with himself, "God, I thank thee that I am not like other men, extortioners, unjust, adulterers, or even like this tax collector. I fast twice a week, I give tithes of all that I get." But the tax collector, standing far off, would not even lift up his eyes to heaven, but beat his breast, saying, "God, be merciful to me a sinner." I tell you, this man went down to his house justified rather than the other; for every one who exalts himself will be humbled, but he who humbles himself will be exalted.'"

(Luke 18:9-14)

20

"GOD, BE MERCIFUL"

In the eighteenth chapter of Luke there are two parables on prayer. The first one is about a widow who continued to bother a judge until finally he had to hear her case. In this parable Jesus teaches that His disciples should be as persistent in prayer as the widow was in her complaint. The second parable, which allows us to see two men at worship, is directed against all sorts of pretentious parade in religion. This parable was originally spoken for those "who trusted in themselves that they were righteous and despised others."

The Two Men

This story, like so many of Jesus' stories, brings into view a set of articulate contrasts. There is, first of all, the contrast between the two men who went to the temple to pray. One man was a Pharisee. The name Pharisee stood for one who was separate from others. The Pharisees insisted on the meticulous observance of the law, and they set themselves apart from the ordinary people whom they called "the people of the land." They were strict legalists. They regarded themselves as protectors of the law; they were accused of "building a fence around the law," which meant that they built around the law a wall of their own traditions. They analyzed the law to death. Jesus said they made void the Word of God by their traditions (Matthew 15:6; Mark 7:8ff.).

Numerous illustrations could be given to show how the Pharisees "fenced" the law through their traditions. Take, for example, the matter of the washing of hands. This was considered a religious rite by the Pharisees, and there were very rigid regulations that had to be followed. It was necessary that the water drawn be as pure as possible; it was not to be defiled by using part of it for some other purpose. In each washing the minimum amount of water permissible was a quarter of a *log*, equal to about one and a half eggshells. The water was poured over both hands. In order that the entire hand might be washed, the hands were lifted up to make the water run down to the wrist. After one hand was cleansed, it could be used to rub the other hand. Then followed a second washing, this time the hands being held down to allow the water to drop off of the finger tips. The purpose of the second washing was to rinse away the water that had touched the defiled hands in the first washing.[1]

These pedantic regulations were characteristic of the Pharisees in the first century. So when Jesus describes a Pharisee as going to the temple to worship, a vivid picture comes to our minds. The Pharisee is a supremely religious man. He comes to the temple at the precise hour of prayer. He sweeps up the steps with a lordly look, all eyes watching him. He enters the Court of Israel and draws near to the altar of burnt offering. He stands erect, displays his broad phylacteries, looks around at others, and begins to phrase certain familiar words.

The other man was a tax collector. While the Jews were under Roman domination, there were many taxes they had to pay. There was a land tax, which was payable in produce or money. There was a poll tax and a tax on personal property, which every person had to pay. There were export and import customs, tolls charged at harbors, roads, bridges, city gates, and so forth. To gather these various taxes, the Romans borrowed a method of tax-collecting used by the Ptolemies of Egypt. Instead of sending their own officials in to exact payment, they contracted with others the right to collect taxes. For a given locality a definite sum would be agreed upon, and anything collected above that would go to those who contracted the taxes. These contractors had numerous assistants working for them in the actual collecting of the taxes. The subordinates were the despised publicans or tax collectors mentioned in the New Testament.[2]

Tax authorities are always unpopular, and this was especially so for the tax collectors in the land of Palestine. The proud Jewish people deeply resented their being subjects of Rome. Radical factions among them maintained that to pay tribute to Caesar was to commit treason against God. Thus tax collectors were not merely the representatives of a foreign government; in the eyes of many Jews they had sold themselves out to the oppressor, and this they had done at the expense of their own countrymen. Besides, the

---

[1]Alfred Edersheim, *The Life and Times of Jesus the Messiah*, II, 10-12.
[2]See the articles "Tax, Taxes," "Tax Collector" in *The Interpreter's Dictionary of the Bible* (New York: Abingdon Press, 1962), IV, 520-22.

tax collectors were notoriously dishonest. Many of the people did not know the tax laws, and often under the guise of some unread law the tax collectors would literally steal everything they had. To be a tax collector, therefore, was to be counted as the lowest and meanest of all sinners.

So the two men who went into the temple were at opposite poles. The Pharisee was on the top rung of the social ladder, the tax collector was at the bottom. One man was respected and honored, the other was an outcast, a traitor and a robber. How amazing it is, then, that Jesus dared to compare them. And how revealing the comparison is as we overhear their prayers.

The Two Prayers

The Pharisee took his customary position and, with raised chin, spoke words that laid bare his inner self. "God, I thank thee that I am not like other men, extortioners, unjust, adulterers, or even like this tax collector. I fast twice a week, I give tithes of all that I get." What kind of prayer is this? Why was it uttered in vain?

1. *The Pharisee's prayer was a prayer of imperfect goodness.* Much of it consisted of negative goodness. The man found pleasure with himself because of certain things he had not done. He was not guilty of extortion, nor was he dishonest or immoral. Even his fasting and tithing were in a sense negative, for these were things that he had given up. Thus the Pharisee lived by the negative of the Golden Rule. It was the accepted rule of life at that time. Rabbi Hillel, who died in the beginning of the Christian era, had done much to popularize it. Once a Gentile came to him and said that he would become a proselyte if he could teach him the whole law while standing on one leg. Rabbi Hillel, shifting his weight to one foot, answered: "Do not to thy neighbor what is disagreeable to thee."[3] Living by this rule the Pharisee had become quite self-satisfied. His negative religion had left him content with himself, and he was perfectly sure that if anybody had gained heaven it was he. In addition, he made the mistake of measuring himself by the other fellow. He was always scrutinizing others. It is significant that as he prays his eyes rove about until he sees the tax collector. As compared with him, of course, he is a saint. It was not much to his credit that he was better than a tax collector. By the cheap method of making others look bad, he made himself look good. But he was the loser, for he was blinded to his sinful self.

---

[3]Cited by Schaff, *History of the Christian Church*, I, 161.

2. *The Pharisee's prayer was a prayer of pride.* His first words are that he is thankful for not being like other men. What an odious way to begin a prayer! It is as much as to say, "Look at me, God, what a splendid person I am!" He speaks not out of gratitude, but as though he would invite God to join in admiration of himself. There was nothing in his prayer but "I." He was only concerned with what "I" had done and not done. He could list all the things under the sun that he had not engaged in. He could boast that he fasted twice a week. The Pharisees usually fasted on Mondays and Thursdays, for Moses was supposed to have ascended Mt. Sinai on a Monday and descended on a Thursday. To fast twice a week was much more than the minimum requirement; according to the Jewish law, the Day of Atonement was the only day in the year that demanded a fast. The Pharisee could also boast that he gave tithes of everything he acquired. Undoubtedly this included tithes of petty things, like herbs of mint and dill (see Matthew 23:23). Even the tithing of trifles contributed to his conceit. He was very proud that he had not omitted keeping the least of the commandments. Therefore, this is why he does not in all of his prayer ask a petition of God. Does he seek the pardon of his sins? Does he ask for divine strength or guidance? No! He sees the publican over in the corner of the temple court. Does he pray for him? Absolutely not! He does not ask because he is in want of nothing. *He does not need God.* It is little wonder, then, that Jesus introduces him by saying that "he prayed with himself." He spoke in the circle of "I." Separated from others and separated from God, his prayer did not reach the roof of the temple.

How refreshingly different is the prayer of the tax collector. He has not darkened the door of the temple in years. He does not come now for show. He is in trouble. He needs help. He must go to God. But he is not sure that he will be heard. He stands far removed from the altar, with his head dropped between his shoulders. He will not cast a glance to heaven. In sorrow and agony he beats his breast. What can he say? How shall he begin to express the feeling in his soul? — Finally he cries, "God, be merciful to me a sinner!" In the Greek language the definite article is attached to *sinner*, not *a sinner*, but *the sinner*. He regards himself as the worst of sinners, *the* sinner of sinners. His prayer was not a long prayer, only seven words; but it went to the heart of the matter, and was unsurpassably sincere.

The Two Results

As the two prayers were different, so the results of the prayers were different. Jesus pronounces judgment on the men. "I say to you," speaking with His characteristic authority, "this man [the tax collector] went down to his house justified rather than the other." One man was justified, the other was not. One prayer went up like incense before God; the other like a cold wintry wind was blown back in the face of its offerer. In the temple, in the presence of God, the Pharisee had stood, and had gone away "unhelped and unblessed." He went home with the same dead heart as he had before. The next day probably found him once again in the temple praying with himself, self-praised and self-condemned.

It was not a prayerless prayer that the tax collector expressed. He had gone up to the temple because he needed to go. Things were not right, and he wanted to make them right. He came to establish a right relationship with God, and, according to Jesus, that relationship was established. He went home relieved, forgiven, cleansed. He had prayed like the psalmist:

> Evils have encompassed me without number;
> My iniquities have overtaken me till I cannot see;
> They are more than the hairs of my head;
> My heart fails me.
>
> (Psalms 40:12)

He had prayed as Ezra had prayed: "O my God, I am ashamed and blush to lift my face to thee, my God, for our iniquities have risen higher than our heads, and our guilt has mounted up to the heavens" (Ezra 9:6). He had prayed the simple prayer that all men need to pray, "God, be merciful to me *the* sinner!"

> Two men went to pray; or rather say,
> One went to brag, the other to pray;
> One stands up close, and treads on high,
> Where th' other dare not send his eye.
> One nearer to the altar trod,
> The other to the altar's God.

THE PARABLE OF THE LABORERS IN THE VINEYARD

"Then Peter said in reply, 'Lo, we have left everything and followed you. What then shall we have?' Jesus said to them, 'Truly, I say to you, in the new world, when the Son of man shall sit on his glorious throne, you who have followed me will also sit on twelve thrones, judging the twelve tribes of Israel. And every one who has left houses or brothers or sisters or father or mother or children or lands, for my name's sake, will receive a hundredfold, and inherit eternal life. But many that are first will be last, and the last first.

"'For the kingdom of heaven is like a householder who went out early in the morning to hire laborers for his vineyard. After agreeing with the laborers for a denarius a day, he sent them into his vineyard. And going out about the third hour he saw others standing idle in the market place; and to them he said, "You go into the vineyard too, and whatever is right I will give you." So they went. Going out again about the sixth hour and the ninth hour, he did the same. And about the eleventh hour he went out and found others standing; and he said to them, "Why do you stand here idle all day?" They said to him, "Because no one has hired us." He said to them, "You go into the vineyard too." And when evening came, the owner of the vineyard said to his steward, "Call the laborers and pay them their wages, beginning with the last, up to the first." And when those hired about the eleventh hour came, each of them received a denarius. Now when the first came, they thought they would receive more; but each of them also received a denarius. And on receiving it they grumbled at the householder, saying, "These last worked only one hour, and you have made them equal to us who have borne the burden of the day and the scorching heat." But he replied to one of them, "Friend, I am doing you no wrong; did you not agree with me for a denarius? Take what belongs to you and go; I choose to give to this last as I give to you. Am I not allowed to do what I choose with what belongs to me? Or do you begrudge my generosity?" So the last will be first, and the first last.'"

(Matthew 19:27-30; 20:1-16)

21

UNDESERVED FAVOR

We are confronted here with the most puzzling of all the parables. The story, on the face of it, is very improbable; and were it not told by Jesus, we would hesitate to believe it. The owner of a vineyard went out early in the morning looking for workers. Finding some men available, he talked with them, and they agreed to work for a denarius each. The denarius was a Roman coin worth about twenty cents and was the ordinary pay for a day laborer. In all of this there is nothing unusual, for in Palestine a man was hired at dawn and paid at sunset. The early morning hours passed; and because there was much work to be done, the owner goes again to the market-place in search of laborers. According to the story, he finds men at the third, the sixth, the ninth, and the eleventh hours. The Jews divided the daytime into twelve equal parts. The length of the hour depended on the length of the day. The third hour would be approximately 9:00 A.M., the sixth hour about noon, the ninth hour mid-afternoon, and the eleventh hour about 5:00 P.M. It is important to notice that as the owner contacts the different laborers through the day, no bargain on pay is reached with them. The owner simply says that he will treat them right at the end of the day. It is also important to notice that the owner hires all the men he finds, and that none of the men when found refuse to go into the vineyard. They evidently did not feel that they were in a position to bargain; they only wanted a chance to work, and they were willing to commit themselves to the goodness of the owner.

It is at the close of the day that we come face to face with the eccentric lord. The law of Moses stated that a hired man was to be paid at the day's end. Speaking of the laborer, the law read: "You shall give him his hire on the day he earns it, before the sun goes down" (Deuteronomy 24:15; see also Leviticus 19:13). So the laborers were called and given their wages; and, strangely, those who had come into the vineyard last were paid first. Not only so, but the five o'clock men were paid for the full day's work. How surprised and happy they were! What had been a long, fruitless day, as they looked for work, has now been turned into joy by a generous lord. The others employed at different hours were likewise well-treated: they were paid in full, although they had only worked in part. Then the time came to pay those who had worked the entire day. Since the lord had been so gracious, paying as much as a denarius for one hour's work, they expected to get more. But they, too, received the same wages. With bitterness they object, "Have we not borne the burden of the day and the scorching sun? Why have you not been as liberal with us as with the others?" The answer flew back, "I do you no wrong. You have what we agreed upon; take your money and go."

Was the Owner Unjust?

What strikes us first about the parable is that apparently the owner of the vineyard was unjust. We are ready to argue that the men who labored in the heat of the day ought to be paid more than the late-comers. We instinctively have a kind of pity for the grumblers. In order to justify, therefore, the unusual actions of the owner, various explanations have been proposed. It has been said, for example, that the owner's conduct can be explained on the grounds that the late workers did as much in one hour as the early workers did in twelve. But there is no hint of this in the parable. Others have sought to explain the difficulty by assuming that some workers were paid with a brass denarius, and others with a silver or gold denarius. But this interpretation contradicts the parable itself, for we may be sure that no objection would have been forthcoming had each of the early workers received a gold denarius. Thus we must look elsewhere for the correct explanation. It must be granted that all the workers were not treated on the same basis. The owner himself acknowledges this. "Am I not allowed," he asks, "to do what I choose with what belongs to me?" But if the owner's methods represented unequal treatment, they did not represent unfair treatment. He did not wrong the early workers by doing a favor to their fellows. He did not withhold from them one cent of what was theirs. The trouble with the early workers was that they were jealous over what the others had received. They simply begrudged the owner's generosity. They murmured not because the lord had deprived them, but because he had been so merciful to the others.

The Original Warnings

It should always be kept in mind that this parable was addressed directly to the apostles. In the previous chapter (Matthew 19), we read of a young man who came to Jesus in quest of eternal life. He was a good man, he had kept all the commandments of the law from his youth. Yet one thing he lacked. Jesus said that he needed to sell whatever he had, give it to the poor, and come and follow Him. The young man, clinging to his many possessions, went away sorrowfully. Then Peter, unaware of his self-righteous pretension, drew a contrast of himself and the apostles with the self-centered rich man. He says, "Lo, we have left everything and followed you. What then shall we have?" Jesus responds that they, and all others who forsake themselves, will be greatly compensated — a hundredfold in this world and eternal life in the world to come. But lest Peter get the wrong impression, Jesus hastens to add, "Many that are first will be last, and the last first." That is to say, "Do not be so much concerned about what you are going to get. In the kingdom of heaven it is not a matter of punching the clock, so much work and so much reward. If that is your attitude, great as your work may be, it will be small in the sight of God. Men may regard you first, but God will regard you last." Then Jesus gives the parable as an illustration of what He meant. The first hired were the last paid and the least honored. Not simply because they were first were they made last, but because *they had the wrong spirit of work.* When so understood, the parable becomes a warning to the apostles who, as the first workers in the vineyard, might through an improper spirit end up as last in the kingdom.

The parable also may be taken as a warning to the Jews. The Jews had for centuries looked upon themselves as the elect people of God. They were bound to God by a special covenant, and they were the exclusive recipients of His special promises. Very early they had entered the Lord's vineyard. All other nations were late-comers. So according to this view, Jesus is saying that the Jews, like the early workers, would resent the gathering in of the Gentiles. Last in time to come into the kingdom, the Gentiles through their service would be made first; and the Jews, who were once first, because of their hatred of others would be made last. Certainly this interpretation has some merit, especially when it is remembered that the parable stands in a series of parables that have to do with the Jews' rejection of God's kingdom.

Attitude toward Work

Aside from its primary applications to the disciples and to the Jewish nation, the parable plainly teaches other basic truths. It tells us that the amount of work accomplished is not as important as the spirit with which the work is done. In the parable we see two types of workers. There are, on one hand, the workers who work for pay. It is specifically said that the early workers *agreed* to work for a denarius a day. This may suggest that there was some bargaining on both sides. At least it means that they did not set to work until definite terms were met. Many people are like that. On almost every job and in practically every business or profession, there are those who work only for pay. They have decided on their vocation or taken their job with one thing uppermost in their minds: "How much am I going to get?" With this one self-absorbed aim they do their tasks. For them work is a duty, a burden that has to be borne; and other than doing what they are told to do, they yield naked nothing. A teacher who teaches for gain, a doctor who is more concerned about collecting his bills than tending his patients, a preacher who first looks at the paycheck before setting out for a new field, are sowing the seeds of decay in a society they profess to serve. Likewise, in spiritual matters, many people work for pay. They want to deal with the Lord on the principle of so much for so much. They picture God as a ledger-keeper who puts down in the credit column so many hours of work and so many deeds done. This was the attitude that Peter had. "Lord, look at the hard lives we've had to live and the sacrifices we've had to make in following you. Now, tell us what we will get." Peter had the hireling spirit, a spirit which if unchanged would cause him to be last in the kingdom.

On the other hand, there are the workers who work without thinking of the pay. The workers employed in the late hours did not require an agreement before entering the vineyard. They depended solely on the generosity of the owner. It was enough for him to say, "Whatever is right I will give you." They did their work, *trusting* that the master would reward them. True Christian service must always be rendered in that spirit. The man who really serves God does not serve for pay. Love seeks no reward. The mother who guards the bed of a sick child does not think of reward. Parents who plan and save and pray for their children do not expect reward. Love secures its joy in bending low to the poor, in speaking words of encouragement to the depressed, and in sharing a comfortable home with a friend. A legendary but beautiful story is related of Thomas Aquinas. While engaged in worship one day, it is said that a heavenly voice addressed him: "Thomas, thou hast written much and well concerning me. What reward shall I give thee for thy work?" Thomas answered, "Nothing but thyself, O Lord." The true Christian does not worry about reward. He leaves it up to God. He knows that to be with God in eternity is the greatest of all rewards.

The Grace of God

In the parable the workers all received the same pay, no matter what hour they went into the vineyard. Those that worked only one hour received pay for a full day. They did not earn it, but still they received it. They received it because the owner was gracious and good. Surely the lesson here is unmistakably clear. We do not earn what God gives us. We do not deserve His long-suffering with us. He does not owe a single one of us His salvation. The English preacher John Newton once said: "When I get to heaven, I shall see three wonders. The first will be to see many persons there whom I did not expect to see; the second will be to miss many whom I did expect to see; the greatest wonder of all will be to find myself there." We work, it is true, but what God gives is not pay. Salvation is a gift of His grace.

Men stand today in the market-place because no one has hired them. It may be that they are very busily engaged — one at the work-bench, another at his farm, another at his desk — but all work besides God's work is idleness. And for those who are at work in the vineyard, the parable lays it down that hard work through the heat of the day does not automatically demand approval when evening comes.

THE PARABLE OF THE TWO SONS

" 'What do you think? A man had two sons; and he went to the first and said, "Son, go and work in the vineyard today." And he answered, "I will not"; but afterward he repented and went. And he went to the second and said the same; and he answered, "I go, sir," but did not go. Which of the two did the will of his father?' They said, 'The first.' Jesus said to them, 'Truly, I say to you, the tax collectors and the harlots go into the kingdom of God before you. For John came to you in the way of righteousness, and you did not believe him, but the tax collectors and the harlots believed him; and even when you saw it, you did not afterward repent and believe him.' "

(Matthew 21:28-32)

22

THE TEST OF TWO SONS

This parable in an extraordinary way reveals Jesus as the Master Teacher. Gathered around Him were a group of black-hearted Jews who were seeking His destruction. For their benefit He told a story, and then He asked their opinion of it. The answer they gave was perfectly correct, unaware of the story's implications. Not until it was finished did they realize that their response had accused themselves and had fixed their own punishment.

The story is about a father who had a vineyard. He went to his two sons and asked them to work for him. The first son bluntly refused, but later changed his mind and went. The second son readily agreed to work, but never kept his promise. "Of the two sons," Jesus asked, "Which did the will of his father?" It was an incisive question that demanded an answer.

The meaning of the parable is crystal clear. The first son who would not work and later decided to work stands for the tax collectors and sinners. All their lives by their wicked deeds they had been saying no to God; yet when Jesus came they could no longer persist in sin but pressed to enter the kingdom. The second son represents the leaders of the Jews, the Pharisees and the Sadducees, who were always making the pretense of serving God, but when Jesus came they despised His teachings and finally crucified Him. They had rejected John, they rejected Jesus. Tax collectors and sinners had turned from their ways, but the Jewish aristocracy had made no amends and had cast aside the heavenly kingdom.

The parable is rich in content and suggests a number of practical lessons beyond its original application. These lessons may be grouped around three ideas: the call, the work, and the workers.

The Call

One of the first things that impresses us in this parable is the direct way the father approaches his sons. He feels that he has the right to ask them to go into his vineyard. He speaks to both in the kindest of terms and says, "Son, go work!" In this way God as Father gently calls all men. It is God who is ever seeking workers; it is God who takes the initiative to bring the inactive and indifferent into His vineyard. Jesus speaks of this divine impulse. He says, pointing to Himself, "No one can come to me unless the Father who sent me draws him" (John 6:44). God *draws* men to the Savior. How does He accomplish this? It is not through a weird dream or a fantastic vision that God reaches men. It is not by the ouija board or the crystal ball. What is His drawing power? Jesus continues and explains: "It is written in the prophets, 'And they shall all be taught by God.' Every one who has heard and learned from the Father comes to me" (verse 45). Thus God draws men through teaching. Paul the Apostle said that men are called by means of the gospel (2 Thessalonians 2:14). Men are brought near the fountain of grace when they learn and receive and obey the gospel of Christ.

It is significant that the father who had only two sons asked each of them to work. God's call goes out to all His children. It is as world-wide as human flesh. It is as all-pervading as human needs. It speaks to the cheerless and downtrodden and says, "Come to me, all that labor and are heavy laden, and I will give you rest" (Matthew 11:28). It summons disciples to evangelize the nations. Not a soul is to be left out. The call is universal, and it is individual. God speaks to you and to you and to me. He bids us one by one. He wants all His children to enter His vineyard, and when one does not enter in, it is a flat refusal to acknowledge His authority.

The Work

What did the father desire his sons to do? He asked them *to work* in the vineyard. The call from God, then, is a call for men to work. It is not a call to rest and ease. Tennyson in his poem "The Lotus-Eaters" retells the story found in the *Odyssey* of Ulysses' visit to an enchanting land that was "always afternoon." There the sailors came and ate of the unusual Lotus plant; and after tasting its sweet fruit, all they wanted to do was to sleep and dream and live with half-shut eyes. And so they say:

> Surely, surely, slumber is more sweet than toil, the shore
> Than labor in the deep mid-ocean, wind and wave and oar;
> O, rest ye, brother mariners, we will not wander more.

They had lost all desire to return to their homeland and were perfectly content to recline on the hills with their dreams. Many people today in Christ's vineyard are like the Lotus-eaters, content to bask in the sunshine of indolence. They do not realize what being a Christian demands. They have entered the Lord's church like people run to a shelter to escape a storm; and when once inside, they just stand around and watch it rain. It is true, of course, that there is a certain measure of safety and protection in the church, and that among God's people one can find much strength for his soul; but the church, like a vineyard, is a place of work, and all of those in the vineyard should be engaged in its program of work. We say that we are Christians, but often we do not spend fifteen minutes during the week working at the job. We say that we are Christians, and yet many times we are too lazy to visit someone who is in the death-grip of sin. It must not be forgotten that the Lord's vineyard is a place where work is to be done.

But the call of the father to his sons had a sense of urgency about it. "Go and work in the vineyard *today*." Work needed to be done, and it needed to be done that day. So Christ's call is for men who will work for Him today. That is, after all, the only time there is. Yesterday is gone forever, and we dare not boast of tomorrow (Proverbs 27:1). Today is all that we have. It is our one chance, our one opportunity to serve. "Behold, now is the acceptable time; behold, now is the day of salvation" (2 Corinthians 6:2). If we hold back and procrastinate, if we wait until tomorrow to do the work of today, the chances are the work will never be done; and in effect we are like the son who bluntly said to his father, "I will not."

The Workers

1. It is interesting to see how the two sons responded to the father's command. One son was very polite and respectful. When asked to work he gives an immediate reply, "I go, sir." Though his brother might refuse his father, he would not. He would go. How courteous he is. And how sure he is that he will succeed.

Why, then, did he fail his father? Why at the end of the day had he not gone near the vineyard? It was not that he had deliberately deceived his father. He had worked out no plot of intrigue by which he hoped to bankrupt his father. He did not purposefully lie to him. He purposed to obey him. In his father's presence he really intended to go to the vineyard, but in his absence he found that the doing of the task was more difficult than the saying of the words.

This son represents, therefore, that large host of Christ's would-be followers who profess much and practice little. Many people, like the son, pledge their loyal service to the Master and then fall down on their pledge. From its earliest times the church has always been plagued by this problem. In the first century there were a group of pseudo-Christians who were called the *Gnostics*. They made great professions. They prided themselves on their fellowship with God, on their walking in the light, on their living above sin. These were glowing words. Yet many of them lived in the depths of sin; no physical appetite or immoral desire was forbidden to them. To counteract such perversity John writes that "God is light, and in him is no darkness at all" and that "he who says 'I know him' but disobeys his commandments is a liar, and the truth is not in him" (1 John 1:5; 2:4). The Gnostics also spoke of knowing God and of loving God, yet they had contempt in their hearts for their Christian brothers. This, John says, they could not do. They must love their brothers (1 John 4:7-21; 3:11-18), and their love must be genuine. John exhorts: "Little children, let us not love in word or speech but in deed and in truth (1 John 3:18). Thus in the early church there were those who praised love but did not practice love.

Profession without practice, promise without performance — these continue to be the greatest enemies of the cause of Christ. Mohandas K. Gandhi, who was born a Hindu, spent much of his life in the study of comparative religions. In Christianity he found many teachings that appealed to him, and many Christian people became his friends. Of these people he often spoke warmly. But in his *Autobiography* he tells of several disappointing visits which he made to a church in Pretoria, South Africa. There he found the people only half-heartedly interested in the Christianity they professed. Of them Gandhi wrote: "The church did not make a favourable impression on me. The sermons seemed to be uninspiring. The congregation did not strike me as being particularly religious. They were not an assembly of devout souls; they appeared rather to be worldly-minded people, going to church for recreation and in conformity to custom. Here, at times, I would involuntarily doze. I was ashamed, but some of my neighbours, who were in no better case, lightened the same.

I could not go on long like this and soon gave up attending the service."[1] It is a sad passage in an immensely interesting autobiography. A man who was to become one of the world's great leaders was hindered in his search for truth by the undesirable lives of those who claimed to be Christians.

2. The other son refused his father and curtly said, "I will not." He offered no reason or excuse. He was not going. Many people are like this son. When the Father calls them to enter His vineyard, they bluntly refuse. They say that they will have nothing to do with any kind of church. They do not excuse their sins. In fact, they speak of their sins freely, as though a frank confession of their immorality can serve as a substitute for their obedience. But in the Last Day what comfort will there be to the lost man who openly traveled the highway to destruction? A man is no less a sinner when he admits that he is not a saint.

The son, however, made a change for the better. He remembered his ugly mood and the blatant discourtesy he had shown his father. He had begun the day badly. But having begun wrong, he saw no reason to continue in the wrong. So he repented. Of what did his repentance consist? It was more than simply a twinge of sorrow because he denied his father. He could have grieved much without repenting. When did he repent? Only when he changed his mind, when he turned in the opposite direction, and when he actually went to work in the father's vineyard!

Which of the Two?

Jesus asked which of the two sons did the will of his father. There is a world of emphasis on the word *did*. Of all things that could be said about them, the only important thing, according to Jesus, is whether the sons *did* the will of their father. All else is of no consequence. No matter how good the intentions, no matter how many the promises, the simple fact is that one son *did* and one son *did not*. Fine words can never take the place of fine deeds.

---

[1]M. K. Gandhi, *Gandhi's Autobiography*. First written in Gujarati under the title *The Story of My Experiments with Truth*; translated by Mahadev Desai. (Washington, D.C.: Public Affairs Press, 1948), p. 198-99.

THE PARABLE OF THE WICKED HUSBANDMEN

" 'Hear another parable. There was a householder who planted a vineyard, and set a hedge around it, and dug a wine press in it, and built a tower, and let it out to tenants, and went into another country. When the season of fruit drew near, he sent his servants to the tenants, to get his fruit; and the tenants took his servants and beat one, killed another, and stoned another. Again he sent other servants, more than the first; and they did the same to them. Afterward he sent his son to them, saying, "They will respect my son." But when the tenants saw the son, they said to themselves, "This is the heir; come, let us kill him and have his inheritance." And they took him and cast him out of the vineyard; and killed him. When therefore the owner of the vineyard comes, what will he do to those tenants?" They said to him, 'He will put those wretches to a miserable death, and let out the vineyard to other tenants, who will give him the fruits in their season.'

"Jesus said to them, 'Have you never read in the scriptures:
"The very stone which the builders rejected has become the head of the corner; this was the Lord's doing, and it is marvelous in our eyes"?

Therefore I tell you, the kingdom of God will be taken away from you and given to a nation producing the fruits of it.' "

(Matthew 21:33-43)

(Parallel passages: Mark 12:1-12; Luke 20:9-18)

23

THE GOODNESS AND SEVERITY OF GOD

When Jesus spoke this parable His hour had come. Throughout His ministry He had spoken of His time and His hour (John 2:4; 7:6, 8; 12:23). All through His life Jesus knew that He had come for a specific purpose and to accomplish a specific work. It was His unique task to bring to consummation the grand purposes of God for a lost world. In His public preaching, however, it would have been disastrous for Him to have announced that He was Messiah. *Messiah* was a term that made all of Palestine bristle with patriotic fervor, that incited head-strong enthusiasts to such heights that they wanted to take up arms and drive the Roman legions out from their country. So it was necessary for Jesus to avoid a public use of the term. But as the time drew near for Him to face death, Jesus talked more freely about His real nature. When finally His hour arrived, with deliberate calculation and according to a set plan, He went to Jerusalem to die. He enters Jerusalem in triumph and is openly proclaimed as Messiah. He goes into the temple and with reckless abandon overthrows the tables of the money-changers. He refuses to tell by what authority He is doing these things. He takes matters into His own hands. And now that He is teaching in the temple, He forces the issue with the Parable of the Wicked Husbandmen.

The Parable

The story that Jesus tells brought familiar pictures to mind in His audience. The land of Judea was a land of many vineyards. According to Jesus' story, the householder took great care in preparing his vineyard. The plot of land was made ready. Large stones were removed and the ground was plowed. The vines were planted, and around it was placed a hedge to protect the vineyard from wild animals and thieves. The hedge was either a thorn hedge or a stone wall. A wine press was made. The ordinary press consisted of two pits which were dug out of rocky ground. The pits, which were connected by a channel, were so constructed that one pit was higher than the other. The grapes were pressed by foot in the higher vat, and the juice was allowed to drain down into the lower. A tower also was built, probably made of stone. It was used to provide lodging for the workers and also as a lookout against possible robbers during the harvest time. Having equipped the vineyard, the householder rented it out to tenants and went away into a far country. In those days Palestine was a troubled land, and it was nothing unusual for a man to leave his property in the care of others and go and live abroad. Rent from the land was derived in one of three ways. The tenant might give a stated amount of money to the owner; or he might pay a certain amount of produce, whether the harvest was good or bad; or he might agree to share in a certain portion of the fruit, usually one-third or one-fourth of the harvest.[1] But in the parable the tenants continually refused to pay their rent. Not only so, but they shamefully wronged the representatives that were sent to them, and at last they murdered the owner's beloved son. There is here also a sad touch of realism in the story, for in Palestine land-renters frequently abused the legitimate rights of absentee landlords. So the story that Jesus told was the kind of story that might take place at any time.

The original meaning of the parable is quite clear. A number of details in the story represent the actual historical situation of the Jewish nation. The householder who planted the vineyard is God; the vineyard is the Jewish nation; the husbandmen who were placed over the vineyard are the priests and elders of the people; the servants that were sent again and again are the prophets of the Old Testament; the son who was cast out of the vineyard and killed is Jesus Christ Himself. Thus the parable is a commentary on God's gracious dealings with His people, His constant pleadings for them to repent, their determination to persist in wickedness, their willingness even to kill Jesus, and their final and irrevocable rejection by God. Jesus asked His hearers what the owner of the vineyard would do to his rebellious servants. The Jews gave a ready response: "He will put those wretches to a miserable death, and let out the vineyard to other tenants who will give him the fruits in their season." Thus speaking, they unwittingly pronounced judgment against themselves.

---

[1] See Alfred Edersheim, *The Life and Times of Jesus the Messiah*, II, 423.

Lessons from the Parable

Too often this parable is read as though nothing is to be seen in it except the doom of the Israelite nation. Certainly this is the main point that Jesus had in mind. When viewed from another standpoint, however, the parable assumes a slightly different character with certain definite lessons.

1. *It teaches us something about Christ.* In the parable Jesus is the son who was sent as the last opportunity for the evil tenants. According to Mark's account, Jesus represents Himself as "a beloved son" and one who is "heir" of "the inheritance" (Mark 12:6-7). As Son He holds a unique place. The other messengers had come as servants. He came not as a servant but as the Beloved Son. Thus Jesus definitely sets Himself apart from other men. His claims here and throughout His ministry were quite extraordinary. He said that He was the Bread of Life (John 6:35), the Light of the world (John 8:12), the Way, the Truth, and the Life (John 14:6). He came, He said, that men might have abundant life (John 10:10). He spoke of Himself as being greater than Jonah and greater than Solomon (Matthew 12:41-42). He existed before Abraham (John 8:58), and even before the world was created (John 17:5). He maintained that He and the Father are one (John 10:30), and, therefore, He said that to see Him was to see the Father (John 14:9). These are stupendous claims, made by Him who is known as the meekest and humblest of men; made without explanation or apology; stated by Him as self-evident truths. These claims cannot easily be written off. They are a part of Him, they explain Him. Without them the whole personality of Jesus is submerged in an eternal enigma. Jesus claimed to be divine; and this parable is one of those passages that sets forth His claim in the clearest possible light.

2. *It teaches us something about men.* In the parable the vineyard planted by the householder had every possible advantage — a hedge, a wine press, a tower, everything that was desirable. In the same way God had made ample provisions for Israel. He brought them out of Egypt and planted them in a good land. He took them to Himself, gave them a written law, and they became His people. He lavished upon them His special concern and surrounded them with special privileges. Yet Israel, the choice among the nations, utterly failed God and did not take advantage of its select position.

One lesson of the parable is that human privileges and human responsibilities cannot be taken lightly. When God makes provision for man, He expects something in return. This is the way it has always been. When times are good as they are now, when human freedoms are many, when the opportunities of living in a great land are so unlimited, God surely expects much of us. In the church our resources of wealth and learning have never been more abundant. Our opportunities to serve mankind and to reach the world with Christ's message have never been so vast. And these opportunities, numerous as they are, transmit to us certain inescapable responsibilities. There is an old legend that tells of how Jesus was received in heaven after His death and resurrection. One of the angels met Him and said, "You must have suffered terribly for men down in the world." Jesus answered, "I did." "But do all men know," said the angel, "how much you loved them and suffered for them?" "No," said Jesus, "only a few men in the land of Palestine know about it." "What have you done," asked the angel, "to let other people know about it?" Jesus answered, "I have told Peter and James and John to tell others, and the others to tell the others, until all men know the story of how much I love them." On hearing this the angel was doubtful. "But what will happen," he said, "if Peter and James and John forget? What if they fail to tell the others? What then?" Back came the response of Jesus, "I haven't made any other plans; I'm counting on them." Peter, James, and John had received privileges that no one else had received; they had seen things that no other man had seen; *and Jesus was counting on them.* Their awesome responsibility has been handed down to us; and with our many advantages and abilities, Christ is surely counting on us.

3. *It teaches us something about God.* In the parable God is the patient householder who is looking for fruit from the vineyard. He sends the first messengers and they are cruelly rejected. He waits. He sends other messengers, and they are likewise rejected. Still He waits. He tries to convict the evil tenants and restore in them a sense of honor. Finally He sends again. God is infinitely merciful and patient with men today. We may wonder sometimes why God is so patient with us. We sin often, we neglect our duties, we fail Him in countless ways. We sometimes think that if we were in charge, we would have brought the world to an end long ago. But God's judgment delays. He does not want a single one to be lost (2 Peter 3:9). He is like the

householder who, after continual rejection, sends His beloved Son in the hope that men will revere Him.

The Greatest Sin

No truth in the Bible, however, is more plain than this: the patience of God can be exhausted with men. There is a limit even to divine grace. In the parable, after the wicked men had killed the Son, no more mercy could be shown. They had filled up the measure of their guilt.

The Jews committed the greatest of sins by rejecting Christ. They had been wayward and stubborn and fruitless for centuries; but their most atrocious crime was to take Him who is Life and nail Him to a cross. For this vile deed they had to pay the eternal consequences. That was their sin of sins. To reject Christ today is still to bring condemnation on oneself. "He who does not believe is condemned already, because he has not believed in the name of the only Son of God" (John 3:18). No man can remain neutral on Christ. Every man to whom the gospel is preached must either believe and follow Him or commit sin by rejecting Him. Luke's account of the parable, speaking of Christ as the stone, concludes with the statement: "Every one who falls on that stone will be broken to pieces; but when it falls on any one it will crush him" (Luke 20:18).

THE PARABLE OF THE TEN VIRGINS

" "Then the kingdom of heaven shall be compared to ten maidens who took their lamps and went to meet the bridegroom. Five of them were foolish, and five were wise. For when the foolish took their lamps, they took no oil with them; but the wise took flasks of oil with their lamps. As the bridegroom was delayed, they all slumbered and slept. But at midnight there was a cry, "Behold, the bridegroom! Come out to meet him." Then all those maidens rose and trimmed their lamps. And the foolish said to the wise, "Give us some of your oil, for our lamps are going out." But the wise replied, "Perhaps there will not be enough for us and for you; go rather to the dealers and buy for yourselves." And while they went to buy, the bridegroom came, and those who were ready went in with him to the marriage feast; and the door was shut. Afterward the other maidens came also, saying, "Lord, lord, open to us." But he replied, "Truly, I say to you, I do not know you." Watch therefore, for you know neither the day nor the hour.' "

(Matthew 25:1-13)

24

"THOSE WHO WERE READY"

Chapter 25 of Matthew presents a series of parables on preparedness: the Parable of the Ten Virgins (verses 1-13), the Parable of the Talents (verses 14-30), and the Parable of the Sheep and the Goats (verses 31-46). The series is an outgrowth of Jesus' discourse to His disciples on the fall of the city of Jerusalem and the time of His second coming (Matthew 24:3ff.). As He spoke of His second advent, Jesus warned that the time would arrive unexpectedly and would find many unprepared. He spoke of faithful and wise servants who did their duty while the master was away. He also spoke of evil servants who, thinking that the master was delayed, were careless and positively wicked in their conduct; and He said that when the master came, he would punish them in the place where "men will weep and gnash their teeth" (Matthew 24:45-51). Immediately following is the statement: "Then the kingdom of heaven shall be compared to ten maidens. . . ." "Then" refers to the great event of the Lord's return.[1] At that time the kingdom will be like the five wise and the five foolish virgins.

The Marriage Feast

Among the Jews the marriage of a boy and girl was looked upon as a matter that affected the entire family. The decision as to whom a son or daughter might marry was made by the parents or guardians. The arrangements were often agreed upon when the couple were still children. As the proposed marriage neared, a formal betrothal ceremony was held. At this time a dowry was paid

[1]It is disappointing to see an able exegete like George A. Buttrick strain to make the parable apply to something else. He holds that the parable does not mainly refer to Christ's second coming; if so, and since He has not come again, the parable "has mocked discipleship for upwards of two thousand years" (George A. Buttrick, *The Parables of Jesus,* p. 236). But the parable cannot be divorced from its context, and the entire context speaks of the coming of the Son of man. Apocalyptic imagery does not argue *per se* for redaction.

to the parents of the bride. The transaction was regarded as final and the betrothal was absolutely binding. If for any reason the marriage did not take place, the girl could not be married to another unless she obtained a legal divorce. The betrothed couple was looked upon as husband and wife, and unfaithfulness on the part of either was considered adultery (Deuteronomy 22:23; Matthew 1:19). Following the betrothal, there was an interval of several months (or a year or so) before the marriage was consummated. What the marriage ceremony consisted of is not known. At the time of the wedding, which usually took place at night, a procession of some sort was held. Generally the friends of the bridegroom went and brought the bride and her attendants to the house of the groom. In the parable, however, the bridegroom is away from home. He is coming from a distance, and no one knows the exact time of his arrival. The maidens in the parable have gathered presumably in the bridal house and are waiting to go out and escort the bridegroom in. They have brought along with them their lamps. The lamps were made of pottery, shaped like a circular, covered bowl. On the side of each lamp a loop-like handle was affixed; at another point on the side there was a small opening where the wick was placed; and on the top was another opening to receive the oil. The kind of oil used in Palestine was the oil taken from the olive tree. The ordinary size lamp was small, so a wise person would supply himself with an adequate amount of oil. Failing to do this, five of the maidens in the parable were marked as foolish. While they were away trying to remedy their mistake, the bridegroom came, the marriage feast began, and the door was shut.

Certain points stand out clearly in the parable. The bridegroom who comes from a distance is Christ; the occasion of His coming is the joyous marriage feast; the time of His coming is unexpected, at midnight when people are heavy with sleep; the maidens who are waiting to go out and meet Him are His professed disciples. The bride is not mentioned because she is not essential to the main theme of the parable.

What Cannot Be Done

Jesus' original audience for this story was His own disciples. It was given as a warning to His own followers, to those who had named His name and considered themselves a part of His own group. Dangers threaten the good as well as the godless. To His disciples, therefore, Jesus gives in this parable certain definite warnings. There are certain things that His disciples cannot afford to do.

1. *We cannot neglect preparation and be ready at His coming.* The foremost lesson of the parable is stated in these words: "Watch therefore, for you know neither the day nor the hour." The key word is "watch." What does this mean? How are Christians to watch for their Lord's return? It certainly does not mean that they must constantly fix their gaze on the sky, waiting for the first glimpse of His glorious appearance. It does not mean that they must talk of nothing else but His coming. Christians must watch with more than their eyes and their tongues. To watch is to have some forethought for the future, to take some prior precaution, to make some preliminary preparation; and it is to continue in that preparation *always.* This was the very thing that the foolish maidens failed to do. They had their lamps. They brought their oil. They began to wait eagerly. But they did not have enough oil. It never entered their minds that the bridegroom might be delayed. And because of this they were "foolish." They were not ungodly or immoral. They were not hypocrites. They were simply foolish. They did not allow for the possibility of delay; and when the lord finally came, they were unprepared.

One of the most inescapable lessons of life is the necessity of being prepared. Practically everything that is done requires preparation beforehand. It is true of reading, writing, and arithmetic; of buying and selling; of sowing and reaping; of winning and keeping friends. There are certain things in life which, if done at all, cannot be done at the last moment. Preparation is essential, for example, to knowledge. Every classroom teacher knows how big a problem it is to get students to give careful attention to their studies when no special assignment is required. If only students worked as hard throughout the school year as they do the last night before a paper is due or the last hour before the final examination! The typical college classroom, before the bell rings, is filled with laughter and smiles and light-hearted conversation. As the teacher walks down the hall, he can hear the noise of the class. When he enters the room, scarcely a book is open. It is that way day after day — except the day of the final examination. On that day when it is too late, unless there has been previous study, then all is quiet, and every head is in a book. *But the time of examination is not the time of preparation.* No course of study can be mastered on the last night; and if the student is able to press into his brain enough facts to pass the examination, he will not be able to make use of them later when he needs them most.

This principle can be illustrated in other ways. Much preparation is required, for instance, before one takes a trip. If a person is going to travel around the world, he cannot wait until the last minute to get things ready. Many arrangements will have to be made at his business; at home a hundred and one little things must be attended to; all the minutiae to obtain a passport must be complied with; flight reservations and hotel reservations must be secured; sightseeing and excursion trips must be planned. And all of these things cannot be done on the last day. So if preparations need to be made before the time of an examination or before a long journey, surely it is necessary to make preparations for the greatest journey and the greatest examination of all: the journey into the Unseen World and the Final Examination before the Judge of the earth. On the day that Christ returns again, it will be too late to make up for the neglect of previous preparation. Christ will come at an unexpected time; and those are foolish who think that they will be able to buy their oil in the last hour after the shops have closed. The point of this parable is that Christians must be on constant watch for their Lord.

2. *We cannot borrow what must be bought.* Often when we read this parable we are ready to sympathize with the foolish maidens. Why did not the wise give to the foolish? How could they be so stingy and heartless and refuse to share their oil with others in the time of distress? The answer is: *there are some things that must be bought; they cannot be borrowed.* Character is like that. It cannot be loaned from person to person. Character is something that must be developed individually, forged by one's own meditations and by one's own decisions. A great man died the other day. He had lived long and well. Through the years he had planted his roots deep in the soil of proper conduct. He had become a veritable moral force for right. What a pity that his strength of will and his love of goodness could not be transferred to those who were at his bedside. But character cannot be bequeathed. Obedience to God is another thing that cannot be borrowed. Here each one is accountable individually. The husband cannot stand for the wife, nor the wife for the husband. All the faith and dedication in the world of parents is not enough for the children; and all the hope and enthusiasm of a boy or girl cannot suffice for an indifferent father or mother. The plain truth is that God expects personal obedience to His commands because He holds every man person-

ally accountable for what he does. The Apostle Paul declares: "We must all appear before the judgment seat of Christ, so that each one may receive good or evil, according to what he has done in the body" (2 Corinthians 5:10). In that day when men shall stand before Christ, it will be utterly impossible to slip into some empty life all those Christ-like qualities — faith, endurance, courage, obedience, character — needed to pass the supreme test. If these qualities are not individually gained in life, in the here and now, they cannot be imparted in the last hour of desperation. "So each of us shall give account of himself to God" (Romans 14:12).

3. *We cannot recall lost opportunities.* When the bridegroom came, the foolish maidens were out buying oil for their lamps. On returning, they found that the marriage feast had already begun. They missed their one chance. They did not seize their one great opportunity. Every day brings us opportunities that we must not neglect. Opportunities to help others abound around us. They are not only in Alaska and Nigeria. They are here, right at our hands.

> Seek not for fresher founts afar,
> Just drop your bucket where you are. . . .
> Parch not your life with dry despair;
> The stream of hope flows everywhere —
> So under every sky and star,
> Just drop your bucket where you are.[2]

Today we may have before us an open door to do good. If we fail to go through that door, it will shut — shut us out from the joy of serving and shut us in with a selfish heart.

The pathetic truth of the parable is that the failure of the foolish maidens was final. The door was shut, and it was shut forever. How much those girls desired to enter! How long they had looked forward to the marriage of their friend! Yet they could not go in. Outside the banquet room, in the dark, they sob, "Lord, lord, open to us." They were near to a welcomed reception, so near that they could hear the inexpressible joy inside, and yet so far. The exclusion was unalterably permanent.

Centuries later, long after the words of this parable have died out, the question still arises, "When will Christ come again?" That is the wrong question. The moment we think "when" we are in trouble. What should we be concerned about? Only whether or not our lamps are trimmed and burning! The one sure way to be ready on *that* day is to be ready *every* day.

---

[2]Sam Walter Foss, *Opportunity.*

THE PARABLE OF THE TALENTS

" 'For it will be as when a man going on a journey called his servants and entrusted to them his property; to one he gave five talents, to another two, to another one, to each according to his ability. Then he went away. He who had received the five talents went at once and traded with them; and he made five talents more. So also he who had the two talents made two talents more. But he who had received the one talent went and dug in the ground and hid his master's money. Now after a long time the master of those servants came and settled accounts with them. And he who had received the five talents came forward, bringing five talents more, saying, "Master, you delivered to me five talents; here I have made five talents more." His master said to him, "Well done, good and faithful servant; you have been faithful over a little, I will set you over much; enter into the joy of your master." And he also who had the two talents came forward, saying, "Master, you delivered to me two talents; here I have made two talents more." His master said to him, "Well done, good and faithful servant; you have been faithful over a little, I will set you over much; enter into the joy of your master." He also who had received the one talent came forward, saying, "Master, I knew you to be a hard man, reaping where you did not sow, and gathering where you did not winnow; so I was afraid, and I went and hid your talent in the ground. Here you have what is yours." But his master answered him, "You wicked and slothful servant! You knew that I reap where I have not sowed, and gather where I have not winnowed? Then you ought to have invested my money with the bankers, and at my coming I should have received what was my own with interest. So take the talent from him, and give it to him who has the ten talents. For to every one who has will more be given, and he will have abundance; but from him who has not, even what he has will be taken away. And cast the worthless servant into the outer darkness; there men will weep and gnash their teeth." ' "

(Matthew 25:14-30)

(Similar Passage: Parable of the Pounds, Luke 19:11-27)

25

FAITHFUL SERVICE

The Parable of the Talents in Matthew and the Parable of the Pounds in Luke are in many ways quite similar. Each parable tells about a man who journeys to a far country; in each certain amounts of money are given to the servants, for which they are individually responsible; in each the lord, on his return, calls his servants in to settle accounts; in each there are those who have done well and are commended for their service; in each there is one man who, because he was afraid, utterly failed in his duty; and each parable concludes with the statement that the man who has will receive more, and from the man who has not will be taken away even what he has. For these reasons, some commentators maintain that what we have here are two versions of one original parable. But others affirm that the parables are independent of each other. For one thing, the circumstances of the parables are entirely different. According to Luke, Jesus told the story of the pounds "because he was near to Jerusalem, and because they supposed that the kingdom of God was to appear immediately" (Luke 19:11). In Matthew, however, Jesus speaks of the talents as He sits on the Mount of Olives (Matthew 24:3ff.), and this on the third day after His entry into Jerusalem. In Luke Jesus addresses publicly a mixed group that followed Him; in Matthew Jesus talks privately with His disciples. The details of the two parables are likewise quite different. Alfred Plummer, in his learned commentary on Luke, has summarized these differences as follows: "(1) In the Talents we have a householder leaving home for a time, in the Pounds a nobleman going in quest of a crown; (2) the Talents are unequally distributed, the Pounds equally; (3) the sums entrusted differ enormously in amount; (4) in the Talents the rewards are the same, in the Pounds they differ and are proportionate to what has been gained; (5) in the Talents the unprofitable servant is severely punished, in the Pounds he is merely deprived of his pound. Out of about 302 words in Mt. and 286 in Lk., only about 66 words or parts of words are common to the two."[1] And then Plummer adds: "An estimate of the probabilities on each side seems to be favourable to the view that we have accurate reports of two different parables, and not two reports of the same parable. . . ."[2]

Distinct as it is from the Parable of the Pounds, the Parable of the Talents serves as a perfect complement to the Parable of the Ten Virgins. In the preceding story the maidens are pictured as *waiting* for their lord; in this story, the servants are represented as *working* for their lord. One stresses the duty of constant alertness, the other the duty of faithful service. Put together both teach the Christian that as he watches he must not be idle, that the best way to be ready is to be busy in the Master's business.

The Entrusted Talents

As Jesus' story goes, before the master left home to go to another country, he called all of his servants in and gave each of them a definite sum of money. The amount of money put in their care varied, depending on the ability of the servants, but in each case the kind of money involved was the talent. The talent in Biblical times was no small sum. Originally it was not a coin but a measurement of weight, equal to about seventy-five pounds. In the time of Jesus one talent was worth nearly a thousand dollars. The servants in the story were actually slaves, the owner's property as much as the money placed in their charge. On returning from his journey, the master called his servants in. Obviously he expected them to put his money to good use while he was away, and this they understood. The first two servants had done well, for they had doubled the amounts given them. The third servant, putting off seeing his master to the last, turned his money back without any increase. His excuse was that he knew his master was a hard man, and so fearing that he would displease him, he slipped out and buried his gift in the ground. The servants who did well were praised, but the servant who failed was excluded from further service and was flung into the outer darkness.

Lessons from the Talents

Some interpreters see the unprofitable servant in this parable as the main character of the story. They maintain, therefore, that the

[1] Alfred Plummer, *A Critical and Exegetical Commentary on the Gospel According to St. Luke,* p. 437.
[2] *Ibid.*

unprofitable servant represents the scribes and Pharisees and the other Jews who would not run the risk of giving full-fledged allegiance to Christ. Possibly there is some merit to this interpretation. But it must be remembered that when this parable was spoken, none of the outside Jews were present, that Jesus' intimate disciples were His sole audience. The primary application of the parable, then, must be to the disciples rather than to the Jews at large.

The lessons of the talents focus attention upon three scenes.

1. *The gifts.* The parable opens with a description of the distribution of gifts: "For it will be as when a man going on a journey called his servants and entrusted to them his property; to one he gave five talents, to another two, to another one, to each according to his ability." The first thing that strikes us here is that each man received something. Not a single servant was passed over, no one left the master's chamber with empty pockets. This is true of all of us. No person responsible to God is left out in the divine distribution of gifts. Each person receives something. Indeed, each person receives much. Even the one-talent servant received the large sum of a thousand dollars. So God has a work for every man, and God gives to every man enough capital to accomplish the work that He intends for him to do.

But each servant, though he received something, did not receive the same gift. To one was given five talents, to another two, and to another one. Each man was given an amount in keeping with his ability. That is the way God acts. He does not expect of us what we cannot do. Our native abilities differ. Some of us are born with strong and active bodies, while others enter the world in poor health, with inherited susceptibility to certain diseases. A few are gifted with superior intellects, many others with something less. Also, our opportunities to develop our gifts differ. A boy brought up in the outdoors is more likely to attain to his physical maximum than a boy restricted to the neighborhood of a big city. In spiritual matters, young men and young women in a small congregation often grow rapidly to Christian leadership, where in a large congregation they may fail to grow because they feel that they are not needed. And even after our gifts have been developed, our opportunities to use them may not be the same. Now there are, of course, always opportunities to serve, but for some the opportunities may not be as many as for others. Not all fields at one moment are glowing with a golden harvest. There are some fields where the ground needs to be prepared; there are other fields that are waiting for the sowing; and, to be sure, not all fields when sown are capable of producing the same crop. So our opportunities, like our innate endowments, vary from person to person. These comprise the "talents" which the Lord gives us. The talents are not just our natural abilities, for the talents are given to each individual according to his ability. All of what God gives to men to perform His tasks are included in the talents.

2. *The use of the gifts.* What was the result of the master's confidence in his servants? To what use did they put his money while he was away? The servants who received the larger sums immediately went to work. They invested their money in profitable enterprises and succeeded in doubling their fortunes. We are not to think that such eminent success came to them without trial. How many must have been the times that they thought of recklessly spending their master's money, or that they teased with the idea of sitting back and playing it safe? Temptations come to the five-talent man as well as to the one-talent man. Now are we to think that the success of these servants was due to an unusual run of luck. Only for one reason were they successful, and that because of hard work.

While two of the servants attained greatness, the other servant followed a path that ended in bleak failure. Why did he fail? Why did he bring shame upon himself and disappoint his master? It was not that he purposed to fail. He doubtless left his master's presence with the firm intention to justify the confidence that had been placed in him. Nevertheless, he failed. There are several reasons for his failure. First, he failed because he did not have faith in himself. He was unsure of his own abilities. When he compared his gift with the larger gifts, he was afraid that he could not do as much as his fellow servants. Not wanting to do the least, he decided to do nothing. Some people are that way. If they cannot have the leading part, they want no part at all; if they are not able to do some really big thing, and gain the approval of their fellows, they will do nothing at all. Sometimes churches that are small make the mistake of thinking that because they cannot support many missionaries abroad, they cannot share in the support of one. Yet each congregation, no matter what its size, has some responsibility in reaching out to a lost world. How many times we, like the one-talent man, fail without giving it a try!

Second, this man failed because he did not have courage to work. His master called him a *slothful* servant. He was afraid of work. Again and again we see that this is the cause of most failures in life. If a man does not work, if he is not willing to pay the price in hard labor, he will never be crowned with success. The same holds true with spiritual things. God has bestowed His grace upon us, but we can multiply our talents in His service only by work.

Third, he failed because he did not have faith in his master. He thought that he would get a bad deal. He pictured his lord as a hard man. Some people look upon God in the same way. Some conceive of God as a stern Power that either is making unreasonable demands or is pushing people around to get His own way. If this is so, if God is like an exacting taskmaster that never lets up, this is all the more reason why we should strive to use the talents He has given us. But, of course, this view of God is utterly untrue. He does not simply order and demand. He loves and pities and extends His arms in mercy. When He gives us a task, He gives us the means to accomplish the task; and He never requires of us something that we have not first been given.

3. *The consequences of using and not using.* The parable tells what happened when the master returned home. There was a time of reckoning. Each servant was summoned in to account for his conduct. The man who had received five talents had gained five more. "Well done, good and faithful servant," says the master. The two-talent man had gained two other talents. His master said to him, "Well done, good and faithful servant." In each case the words of commendation were precisely the same. The master was equally pleased with the service of both. And for them there was a twofold reward. The first was that they would be given even more than they had. "You have been faithful over a little, I will set you over much. . . . For to every one who has will more be given, and he will have abundance." The second reward was that they were admitted into the joy of their lord. This meant that they were granted the right to sit at their lord's banquet table. It was a privilege that slaves never received and one which, perhaps, automatically gave them their freedom.

But the idle servant was forbidden to share the joy and honor at the master's table. And besides, all that he had was extracted from him. His one talent was put into the hands of the man with ten talents. Is that not evidence that his master was harsh? No; it is the inevitable consequence of doing nothing. It is a law of life that *we lose what we fail to use.* It may be that a person has some special ability. As he uses that ability day after day, his ability increases; if he does not use it, his efficiency in that thing will diminish to nothing. A new word, a new name, a new story not quickly repeated is soon forgotten. Any artistic skill or athletic dexterity requires constant sharpening. So in the spiritual realm every gift given by God must be put to work or else it will be taken from us.

What was the difference between the servants? Why were two profitable and one unprofitable? The answer lies not in the fact that the two from the beginning were more gifted. With all their ability they still could have been lazy and buried their talents. It was not because they were brilliant or because they had a knack for business that they were commended. They were commended simply because they had been *faithful* in the service of their absent lord. Each man, with the ability that he possessed, had done his best. When we, too, turn to the Eternal Home, it may be that some will come with arms full of trophies, and that others will come with not as many; but the Lord will run out to meet us with the only words that count, "Well done, good and faithful servant."

THE PARABLE OF THE SHEEP AND THE GOATS

" 'When the Son of man comes in his glory, and all the angels with him, then he will sit on his glorious throne. Before him will be gathered all the nations, and he will separate them one from another as a shepherd separates the sheep from the goats, and he will place the sheep at his right hand, but the goats at the left. Then the King will say to those at his right hand, "Come, O blessed of my Father, inherit the kingdom prepared for you from the foundation of the world; for I was hungry and you gave me food, I was thirsty and you gave me drink, I was a stranger and you welcomed me, I was naked and you clothed me, I was sick and you visited me, I was in prison and you came to me." Then the righteous will answer him, "Lord, when did we see thee hungry and feed thee, or thirsty and give thee drink? And when did we see thee a stranger and welcome thee, or naked and clothe thee? And when did we see thee sick or in prison and visit thee?" And the King will answer them, "Truly, I say to you, as you did it to one of the least of these my brethren, you did it to me." Then he will say to those at his left hand, "Depart from me, you cursed, into the eternal fire prepared for the devil and his angels; for I was hungry and you gave me no food, I was thirsty and you gave me no drink, I was a stranger and you did not welcome me, naked and you did not clothe me, sick and in prison and you did not visit me." Then they also will answer, "Lord, when did we see thee hungry or thirsty or a stranger or naked or sick or in prison, and did not minister to thee?" Then he will answer them, "Truly, I say to you, as you did it not to one of the least of these, you did it not to me." And they will go away into eternal punishment, but the righteous into eternal life.' "

(Matthew 25:31-46)

26

IF ONLY WE HAD KNOWN

The two foregoing parables especially concern Christians, those who are waiting to go out to meet the Bridegroom and those who, while waiting, are engaged in the service of their Lord. This parable, however, envisions all men, for it tells of a final and irreversible judgment of the whole world. For this reason it is more than a parable: it is a realistic prediction of the future in which all nations are brought before the Son of man (see Revelation 20:12-13). Jesus Himself is the Son of man, and in keeping with His Father's wish He proceeds to judge the nations (see John 5:22-23; Acts 17:30-31). He makes division among them like a shepherd who separates the sheep from the goats. In Palestine the task of distinguishing between them was not difficult, for the sheep were white and the goats were black. He places the sheep at His right hand, the position of distinction and honor (1 Kings 2:19; Acts 2:33-34). The goats He turns aside and puts on His left hand. Then the awards are announced. To the righteous the Son says, "Come, inherit the kingdom prepared for you from the foundation of the world." All their lives they had lived in sympathy and self-sacrifice. Now the kingdom that was theirs in God's eternal purpose was to be theirs in actual possession. But the very characteristics that won for them the King's approval were the same characteristics, when absent, that caused the others to be rejected. Those on the left hand had shown no pity and had practiced no self-denial. The kingdom prepared for them was not to be theirs, nothing was to be theirs except a hell ready for the devil and his angels.

Giving to Others

This parable has through the centuries been interwoven into the basic texture of Christianity. How often a Christian is defined in the very terms of this passage, a person who visits the sick, clothes the needy, gives food to the hungry and offers drink to the thirsty.

The reason why these things are so often remembered is because Jesus made them in this scene the standard of judgment for right conduct, the final proof as to whether a man is really *His* disciple. In that Day it will not be a question of how much we know, what creed we can recite, or how many theological definitions we can unravel. It will not even be how good we have been in our morals and ethics. But it will be a question of how much good we have done, a question of how well our deepest feelings have been expressed by the positive action of giving to others. One of the famous preachers of the past explicitly made it known to his congregation that when the gifts to the poor were no longer sufficient, its sacred vessels would be melted down to supply the deficiency. The really important thing, according to Jesus, is how we have responded to the needs of our brothers.

Giving in Simple Things

There are countless lessons in this parable. Jesus here not only enforces the principle of giving, but He puts the principle within the reach of all. In every case we see that the help given was a simple thing. Many times we ask ourselves, "What can I do to help others?" And we conclude, because we are not trained to be missionaries, because we cannot give thousands of dollars to send others to go, that what we can do is too little and therefore we do nothing. Yet what the righteous did in this parable is what every man can do. How important is one act of invitation to a man who does not know Christ! William Barclay retells a story told by Alexander Whyte, the famous preacher of Edinburgh.[1] A business man by the name of Rigby used to stop regularly at Edinburgh. Rigby was by no means a preacher; he could hardly talk to anyone about religion. But one thing he did: each Sunday when he was in Edinburgh he went to church, and each Sunday he did his best to bring someone with him. One day he invited a young man to go with him. The man stubbornly refused, but Rigby insisted and finally the young man agreed to go. As a result of the morning service, the young man wanted to attend again in the evening. And that night he decided to give himself to Christ. The next morning Rigby passed by Whyte's house. He had never met Whyte, but on a sudden impulse he decided to stop and get acquainted with him. Rigby told him about the young man; and Whyte was

---

[1]William Barclay, *And Jesus Said: A Handbook on the Parables of Jesus*, p. 121.

glad to hear it because he felt that his sermon the night before had fallen flat. "What did you say your name was?" Whyte asked. "Rigby," said the man. "Man," said Whyte, "you're the man I've been looking for for years." He then turned and went back to his study and brought out a bundle of letters. All of the letters were the same, telling of how a man by the name of Rigby had invited them to church, and of how as a result, their whole lives had been changed. Whyte told Rigby that twelve of the letters were from young men, and that four of them had already entered the ministry. It was not a large thing that Rigby did, but with the blessing of God his efforts brought much fruit.

Giving without Reward

We note in this parable also that those who had done so many good deeds were quite unaware of their goodness. They had performed their acts of love and mercy unsolicited. Their kindness was spontaneous. And they are greatly surprised at the end when the King so richly rewards them. That is the way giving should always be, unasked and unconcerned about praise. Jesus was constantly emphasizing this point. There were the Pharisees who gave for the glory of themselves. They practiced their *piety in order to be seen by men* (Matthew 6:1).[2] Thus Jesus declared that they had all the reward they were going to get. The Greek verb here is *apecho*. In New Testament times it was a very familiar term. It was the ordinary word that was used on a receipt, to show that a debt had been *paid in full*.[3] So Jesus says that those who give to honor themselves receive their *full payment* in human praise. They gain no other reward.

Our giving today must be such that the left hand does not know what the right hand is doing (Matthew 6:3). This statement of Jesus can be misunderstood. It does not teach "secret giving," as though it is necessary to slip our gifts into the collection plate while no one is looking on. For the right hand to give without the left hand knowing it, refers to our *motives* in giving. That is to say, the right hand should give so unpretentiously, with so little

---

[2]The Greek construction *pros to theathenai* is very emphatic, an articular infinitive of purpose. This is translated very well in the Revised Standard Version.

[3]See Arndt-Gingrich, *A Greek-English Lexicon of the New Testament and Other Early Christian Literature*, p. 84. Paul's statement "I have received full payment" (Philippians 4:18, Revised Standard Version) is an excellent rendering of *apecho*.

desire for credit, that the left hand does not even know what it is doing. There is a beautiful story of an old saint who was offered anything he desired because he had done so many good deeds. His only request was that he might be granted the ability to do good without knowing that he was doing good. And so it happened that wherever he went his shadow cast a blessing after him. The righteous in the parable had done good, but they scarcely remembered it.

Giving to Christ

But the most remarkable thing in this parable is that the people who gave so generously did not know that they were really giving to Christ. They say, "Lord, when did we see you hungry or thirsty or naked? When did we see you ill or in prison? When we did those deeds, when we gave food to that starving man, when we took that stranger in, when we took care of that sick person through the night, *we didn't know that was you.*" "Inasmuch," says Jesus, "that you did it to the least of my brothers, you did it to me." What a startling revelation it was for them to learn that they had actually ministered to Christ.

This parable poses a situation that every person needs to contemplate: "Suppose Christ was on earth today. What would be my attitude toward Him. How much would I be concerned about Him? What kind of treatment would I give Him?" We are ready to answer, being quite liberal with ourselves, that we would be very much interested in Him. We would not neglect Him. Certainly we would not mistreat Him. But, of course, Christ is not here today in flesh and blood. However, and this is a matter that we too often forget, His brothers *are* here, and *whatever we do for them we do for Him.* We may think of it like this. God, the Almighty One, does not need any one of us. Because He is God, He does not need a single thing that we might give Him. Yet God is also a Father, and all men are His children. And the God who in one sense we can do nothing for, in another sense we can do everything for by loving and providing for His children. The only way that we can do anything for God is to do something for His children.

On the other hand, what will God's attitude be toward us if we fail to help His children? Clearly, if we fail them we fail Him. This was the very thing that the rejected could not understand. They say, "Lord, when did we see *you* hungry or thirsty or ill or in prison? When did we see *you* on the streets begging? If we had known that it was *you* in trouble, we would have helped *you!*" We are the same today. We are quite discriminate in our giving. We do not mind helping some dear friend or associate or well-known brother, someone who is our social equal who happened to be overtaken by misfortune. Perhaps we do not mind even giving a meal every now and then to an honest-looking beggar. But to be willing to aid everyone, to treat every person with the same concern and respect that we would have for the Lord Himself, is something that we have not as yet realized in our lives.

It is sad to think that there was a time in the history of earth when men rejected Christ. We find it hard to believe that such a rejection ever occurred. If only we had seen Him as He walked the worn paths of Palestine; if we had heard those words of soft exhortation by Galilee's Sea; if we had witnessed His signs and seen His glory; if we had lived in His time and in His country — no, we would not have denied Him or turned Him away, we would not have marched Him to a cross! But it does not help to say what we would have done had we been there. Jesus came to men then, but He still comes today, to your city and to mine. How do we treat Him? Do we welcome Him? G. A. Studdert-Kennedy of Birmingham, England, wrote:

> When Jesus came to Golgotha, they
> hanged him on a tree;
> They drove great nails through hands
> and feet and made a Calvary;
> They crowned him with a crown of thorns,
> red were his wounds and deep;
> For those were crude and cruel days,
> and human flesh was cheap.
>
> When Jesus came to Birmingham, they
> simply passed him by;
> They never hurt a hair of him,
> they only let him die;
> For men had grown more tender,
> they would not give him pain;
> They only passed on down the street,
> and left him in the rain.
>
> Still Jesus cried, "Forgive them
> for they know not what they do."
> And still it rained the winter rain
> and drenched him through and through;

The crowds went home and left the street
    without a soul to see;
Jesus crouched against a wall
    and cried for Calvary!

And in that Day the lament of many will be the lament expressed in the parable, "Lord, we didn't know that it was you!"

A SHORT BIBLIOGRAPHY

Barclay, William, *And Jesus Said: A Handbook on the Parables of Jesus.* Edinburgh: The Church of Scotland Youth Committee, 1952.

Bruce, A. B., *The Parabolic Teaching of Christ.* New York: A. C. Armstrong & Son, 1894.

Buttrick, George A., *The Parables of Jesus.* New York: Doubleday, Doran & Company, 1928.

Chappell, Clovis G., *In Parables.* New York: Abingdon-Cokesbury Press, 1953.

_____ *Sermons from the Parables.* New York: Abingdon-Cokesbury Press, 1933.

Dodd, C. H., *The Parables of the Kingdom.* New York: Charles Scribners' Sons, 1936.

Findlay, James Alexander, *Jesus and His Parables.* London: Epworth Press, 1950.

Hunter, A. M., *Interpreting the Parables.* Philadelphia: The Westminster Press, 1960.

Jeremias, Joachim, *The Parables of Jesus.* Trans. S. H. Hooke. London: SCM Press, 1954.

Kennedy, Gerald, *The Parables: Sermons on the Stories Jesus Told.* New York: Harper & Brothers, 1960.

Martin, Hugh, *The Parables of the Gospels.* New York: The Abingdon Press, 1937.

Morgan, G. Campbell, *The Parables and Metaphors of Our Lord.* New York: Fleming H. Revell Company, 1943.

Oesterley, W. O. E., *The Gospel Parables in the Light of Their Jewish Background.* New York: The Macmillan Co., 1936.

Smith, B. T. D., *The Parables of the Synoptic Gospels.* Cambridge: University Press, 1937.

Trench, Richard Chenevix, *Notes on the Parables of Our Lord.* Fourteenth Edition, Revised. London: Macmillan and Co., 1882.

Taylor, William M., *The Parables of Our Saviour.* New York: Harper & Brothers, 1886.

Wallace, Ronald S., *Many Things in Parables.* New York: Harper & Brothers, 1955.